1000 FACTS ON
SPORT

First published by Bardfield Press in 2004

Bardfield Press is an imprint of
Miles Kelly Publishing Ltd
Bardfield Centre, Great Bardfield, Essex, CM7 4SL

2 4 6 8 10 9 7 5 3 1

Editor
Kate Miles

Art Director
Debbie [illegible]

Assistant Designer
Tom Slemmings

Picture Research
Liberty Newton

Production
[illegible]

British Library Cataloguing-in-Publication Data
A catalogue record for this book is available from the British Library

ISBN 1-84236-397-2

Printed in China

www.mileskelly.net
info@mileskelly.net

1000 FACTS ON
SPORT

Christopher Rigby

BARDFIELD
PRESS

Contents

Key

Ballsports

Field and track events

Martial arts/Gymnastics

Motorsports

Water and snow sports

Mixed bag

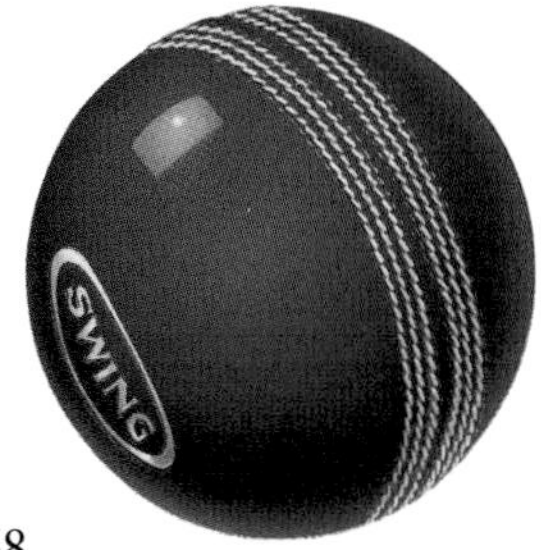
SWING

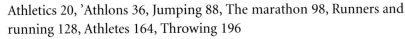

Contents

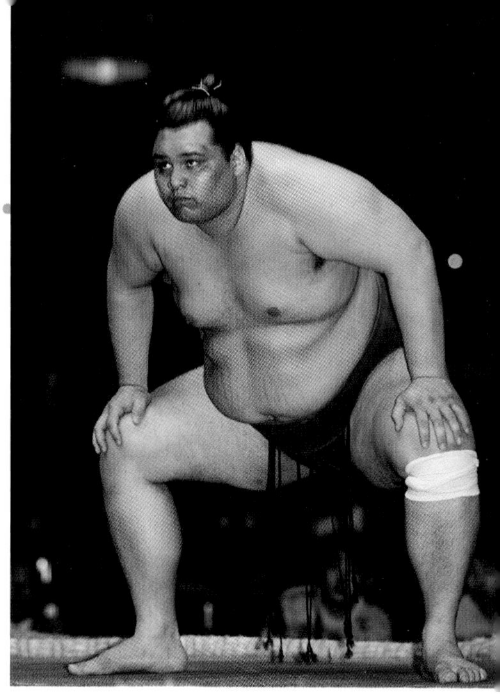

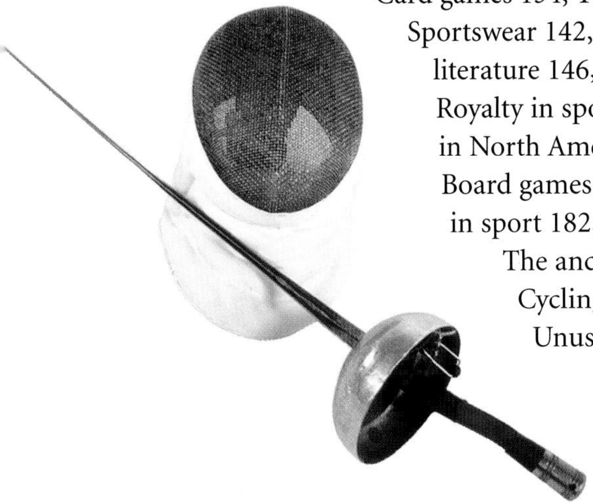

Golf

- **In golf,** one under par is called a birdie, two under par an eagle and three under par an albatross.
- **There are 336 dimples** on a regulation golf ball.
- **Major golf championships** are contested over four rounds of 18 holes making 72 holes in total.
- **A golfer is allowed** to take a maximum of 14 clubs onto the course
- **The word golf** represents the letter G in the NATO phonetic alphabet.
- **In 1899 dentist George F Grant** invented and patented the golf tee.
- **In the 15th century James II of Scotland** banned the game of golf because he believed his subjects were neglecting their archery practice.
- **The Ryder Cup** is a team competition in which American golfers compete against European golfers. It is contested every two years
- **Recent winners** of the British Open are Ben Curtis (2003), Ernie Els (2002), David Duval (2001), Tiger Woods (2000), Paul Lawrie (1999), Mark O'Meara (1998), Justin Leonard (1997).

◀ *The exact origin of golf is unknown, but it was played in Scotland in the 15th century.*

▲ *Tiger Woods has become the most successful golfer since his professional debut in 1997 – winning the Masters tournament.*

FASCINATING FACT

In 1971 astronaut Alan Shepard became the first man to hit a golf ball on the Moon.

Tennis

- **A tennis court is 23.8 m long** and 11 m wide for doubles matches, and 23.8 m long and 8.2 m wide for singles matches. The height of the net is 0.9 m.
- **The tennis term** *love* is derived from *l'oeuf*, the French word for egg, symbolizing a zero.
- **In 1986 yellow balls** were used at Wimbledon for the first time to make them more visible for the TV cameras.
- **Tennis was an Olympic event** from 1896 to 1924 and was reintroduced into the Games in 1988.
- **In 1900 Dwight Davis** gave his name to a team competition between the United States and Great Britain. More than 60 countries now contest the Davis Cup annually.
- **The four tournaments** that make up the tennis Grand Slam are Wimbledon, the US Open, the Australian Open and the French Open.
- **The tennis term** *deuce* derives from *deux*, the French word for two, meaning that an advantage of two points must be gained to win the game.
- **Catgut**, used in the making of tennis-racket strings, is made out of the intestines of various animals (but not cats).

▲ *Tennis is played on different surfaces, such as grass, clay, shale and concrete, but is known as lawn tennis.*

- **A tennis tiebreaker** comes into operation when the set score is six games all.
- **Recent Wimbledon winners** in the men's singles are Roger Federer (2003), Lleyton Hewitt (2002) and Goran Ivanisevic (2001). In the women's singles, Venus Williams won the tournament each year from 2000 to 2002. Justine Henin-Hardenne won in 2003.

▲ *Powerful new rackets with larger heads have added power to the modern game. Top players can achieve speeds of 240 km/h on their serve.*

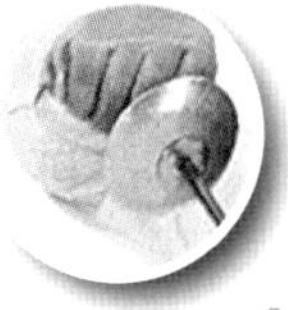

Fencing

- **The strip on which a fencing bout** is fought is called the *piste* and is approximately 14 m long with a minimum width of 1.5 m.
- **Fencers, like footballers**, are issued with yellow and red cards. A yellow card is for a minor offence and a red card results in a point being deducted.
- **At the beginning of a fencing bout** the contestants stand in the *en garde* position and must be at least 4 m apart.
- **Fencers' swords** are attached to their wrists and forearms with a strap called a martingale.
- **A fencing competition** without electronic scoring is known as a dry bout. Four officials, known as the jury, judge these bouts.

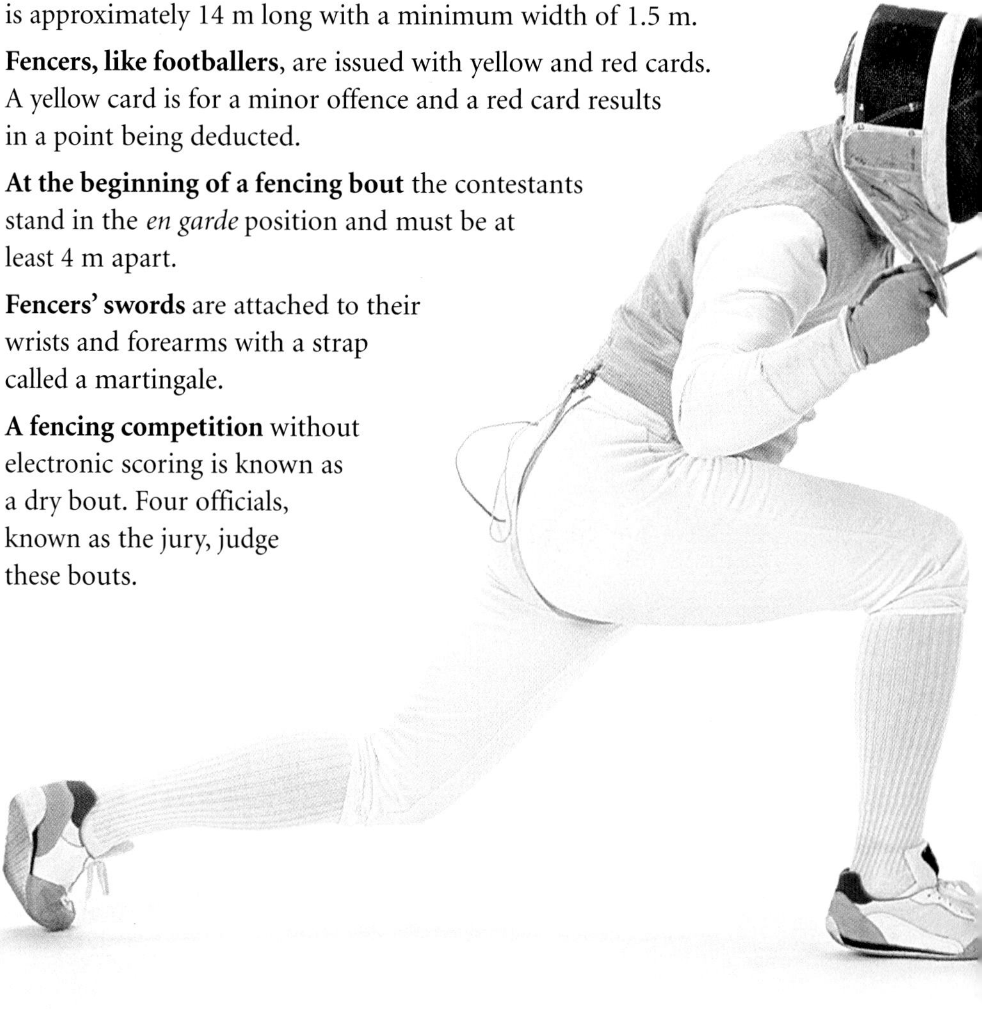

- **The swords** used in fencing competitions are the foil, the sabre and the épée.
- **Before a bout** it is considered polite for a fencer to salute the referee, the audience and the opponent.
- **Fencing has been included** in every modern Olympics since 1896.
- **Fencing is one of the five events** contested in the modern pentathlon.
- **The sport of fencing** is said to have originated in ancient Egypt, to prepare men for war.

◀ *Fencers wear white, tough protective clothing. It must be free from buckles, openings and straps that could cause a sword to snag.*

Rowing

- **In the Olympics** a coxswain must weigh at least 50 kg. If under this weight, he or she must carry sand or weights to make up the difference.
- **In official rowing races** the boat can continue if a rower falls in the water. However, if the coxswain falls out, the boat must stop.
- **In Olympic sculling** the boat must have a minimum weight of 26 kg.
- **At the 2000 Sydney Olympics** British rower Steve Redgrave collected his fifth consecutive Olympic gold medal.
- **In sweep-oared rowing** the rowers use one oar – in sculling the rowers use two oars, one in each hand.

▲ *Steve Redgrave won his fifth Olympic gold medal with team mates James Cracknell, Tim Foster and Matthew Pinsent.*

- **The term** 'catching a crab' means that the oar is stuck in the water, causing the boat to slow down.
- **The sculling race**, The Doggett and Coach Badge, was first contested in 1716 on the River Thames and is still contested annually.
- **In 1912 the *Titanic*** had rowing machines in the gymnasium. As the ship sank, the gym's instructor encouraged the passengers to use them!
- **All Olympic rowing races** for men cover a distance of 2000 m.
- **A rowing first was achieved in 1896** by Norwegians, Gabriel Samuelson and George Horboe, who took 60 days to row across the Atlantic.

▼ *Rowing became a competitive sport in the 18th century. Early boats were very crude in comparison to the sleek designs of today.*

Skating

- **In Olympic competitions** the size of the rink is 60 x 30 m.
- **Speedskaters** wear tight-fitting Lycra suits with aerodynamic hoods in order to reduce air resistance.
- **Ice dancers** receive two sets of marks in competitions, one for technical merit and one for artistic impression, with a maximum score of 6.0.
- **The first ice-skating** world championship was held in St Petersburg in 1896, and was won by a German skater called Gilbert Fuchs.
- **In speed skating** the rules state that competitors have to change lanes after every lap.
- **Figure skating became** an official Olympic sport in 1908, but ice dance had to wait until 1976 before becoming part of the Olympic programme.
- **The figure-skating jump** called the salchow was named after the skating pioneer Ulrich Salchow who won a gold medal at the first-ever Olympic competition.
- **In an Olympic ice dance** competition a panel of nine separate judges mark the skaters.
- **The first ice dancers** to receive a perfect score of 6.0 were Torvill and Dean at the 1984 Olympics.

...FASCINATING FACT...
Ice-skating's patron saint is St Lydwina, a Dutch girl who broke a rib in a skating accident in 1396.

▶ *Ice skating is thought to have developed in Scandinavia, where primitive skates dating back 2000 years have been found.*

Martial arts

- **Grades of proficiency** in judo are known as dans. The highest dan is the tenth dan, which is rewarded with a red belt.
- **The literal meaning** of the word karate is 'empty hand'.
- **Kendo** is fought on a square or rectangular wooden court with sides measuring from 9 to 11 m.
- **A makiwara** is a punching board used in karate training for toughening the hands and strengthening the wrists.
- **Tae kwan do** meaning 'the way of kicking and punching' is the national martial art of Korea.
- **A teacher of Japanese** styles of kung fu is addressed by the title *Sensei.*
- **At the age of 18** the martial arts hero Bruce Lee won a Hong Kong dancing championship for the cha-cha.
- **Kung-fu film superstar** Jackie Chan performs all his own stunts and nearly died making a 16-m jump in the film *Project A* (1984).
- **In the sport of kendo**, fighters wear protective gear called a *bogu* and use a bamboo sword called a *shinai.*
- **There are over 300 styles** of kung fu named after various creatures. These include Monkey, Praying Mantis, Crane and Dragon.

▶ *In judo, contestants wear a judo-gi, a loose-fitting jacket and trousers, and a belt. The suit is made of tough fabric to withstand tugging and pulling and the belt is coloured, denoting grade competence.*

Athletics

◀ *A baton is transferred between teammates in relay races by passing it from hand to hand.*

- **Olympic events**, past and present, in which competitors move backwards include rowing, tug-of-war and the backstroke in swimming.
- **Pole-vaulting** originated in ancient Greece where the Cretan people used long poles to vault over bulls.
- **In discus competition** the marked circle from which the competitor throws has a diameter of 2.5 m.
- **On May 25, 1935** the American athlete Jesse Owens broke six separate world records in the space of a mere 45 minutes.
- **The Olympic motto** of *Citius, Altius, Fortius* means 'swifter, higher, stronger'.
- **Between September 1977 and June 1987** Ed Moses won 122 consecutive races in the 400 m hurdles.

- **The athletics coaches** George Breshnahan and William Tuttle invented starting blocks for sprinters in 1928.
- **In 1968** American sprinter Jim Hines became the first person to run 100 m in under 10 seconds with a time of 9.9 seconds.

- **Over 10,000 athletes** competed in the 2000 Sydney Olympics. The most gold medals were collected by the United States with a total of 39.
- **Stella Walsh** won a 100-m women's gold medal at the 1932 Olympics. She was killed in 1980 during a robbery and an autopsy revealed that she was a man!

◀ *At the Berlin Olympics, US track and field athlete Jesse Owens won four gold medals.*

Fishing

- **In the carp fishing world championship**, the river must have a minimum depth of 1.5 m and a minimum width of 25 m.
- **In the American state of Kansas** it is against the law to catch fish with your bare hands.
- **Fishing** is sometimes called angling because the alternative name for a hook is an angle.
- **All the sturgeon** that are caught in British waters are the property of the Queen.
- **The fishing reel** was invented in 3rd-century China and was inspired by the bobbin used in silk weaving.
- **The first-ever world fly fishing championship** was held in 1981, and in 1987 Brian Leadbetter became the first Englishman to win the title.
- **The patron saint** of fishermen is St Peter.

▶ *There is a great art to tying flies.*

- **Salmon return to the actual stream** where they were born, to breed. This often involves swimming huge distances and overcoming great obstacles to reach their destination.
- **Egg-sucking leech**, Happy Meal and Hairy Dog are just three of the many weird names given to handmade fishing flies.
- **The most ferocious freshwater fish** is the piranha. A group of them can strip an animal as large as a cow within minutes, leaving only the skeleton.

▶ *Freshwater fishing includes game fishing, where members of the salmon family are taken by flies or lures, coarse fishing in which members of the carp family and others are taken by bait or lures and seafishing. Competition angling takes place throughout the world.*

Bowling

- **The standard length** of a ten-pin bowling alley is 19.16 m.
- **Ten-pin bowling** was introduced into the United States because nine-pin bowling was banned. An extra skittle was added to beat the ban.
- **West Indian cricket** star Courtenay Walsh was the first bowler to take 500 test wickets.
- **A perfect score** in a game of ten-pin bowling is 300.
- **Overarm bowling** became legal in the game of cricket in 1864.

▲ *Since the 1960s, tenpin bowling has become a very popular sport worldwide.*

- **Until the 1930s** ten-pin bowling balls only had two holes. A third one was added to give the user a better grip.
- **In cricket, six balls** are bowled in one over and if no runs are scored this is known as a maiden over.
- **In ten-pin bowling** three consecutive strikes is known as a turkey, because bowling alley owners used to give a turkey to any player that achieved this feat.
- **In 1588 the Spanish Armada** was sighted off the English coast. On receiving this information Francis Drake, relaxing during a game of bowls, allegedly said, "We have time to finish our game and beat the Spanish too."

▶ *Special shoes are worn for tenpin bowling. They have white rubber heels and slippery soles for sliding and braking during the approach.*

. . . FASCINATING FACT . . .
The term hat-trick originated in cricket. A bowler who collected three wickets with three consecutive balls received a hat as a reward.

American football

▲ *A team may have as many as 45 players, but only 11 from either team are allowed on the field at one time. Regular substitutions may be made during a game.*

- **In American football** a touchdown is worth six points and a field goal is worth three points.
- **The horizontal bar** of the goalpost in American football stands 3 m from the ground.
- **A desperate pass** thrown a long distance to the end zone in the closing seconds of the game is known as a Hail Mary.
- **Tackling a quarterback** while he is in possession of the ball is known as sacking.
- **In 1948 the Los Angeles Raiders** became the first team to sport a logo on their helmets.

- **An American football game** is divided into four periods of play called quarters, with each quarter lasting 15 minutes.
- **An American football field** is known as a gridiron because of the lines that cross the field at intervals of 4.5 m.
- **In 1972 the Miami Dolphins** scored the lowest ever in a Super Bowl, totalling only three points.
- **The first team** to appear in four consecutive Super Bowls were the Buffalo Bills who achieved this feat from 1991 to 1994, losing all four games.
- **Here are the names** of some of the leading American football teams: the Giants (New York), the Vikings (Minnesota), the Dolphins (Miami), the Bears (Chicago).

◀ *The oval ball is usually a dark red in colour and measures around 28 cm in length.*

The FA Cup

- **Manchester United** won the trophy for a record tenth time in 1999 by beating Newcastle United 2–0 in the final.
- **Premiership clubs** do not enter the FA Cup until the third round, at which stage there are 64 clubs left in the competition.
- **In 1927 Cardiff City** became the only non-English team to win the FA Cup, beating Arsenal 1–0 in the final
- **Recent FA Cup winning captains** are Patrick Vieira for Arsenal in 2003 and 2002, Sami Hypia for Liverpool in 2001, Dennis Wise for Chelsea in 2000, and Roy Keane for Manchester United in 1999.
- **The first-ever FA Cup final** was played in 1872 at Kennington Oval when Wanderers beat Royal Engineers 1–0.
- **In 1923 the first FA Cup final** was played at Wembley, when West Ham lost 0–2 to Bolton. This became known as the White Horse final as a horse called *Billie* helped clear the crowd from the pitch.
- **For the first time in 1967** two London teams lined up to play in the FA Cup final. Tottenham beat Chelsea 2–1.
- **In 2001 Liverpool beat Arsenal** 2–1 in the first FA Cup final to be played in the Millennium Stadium, Cardiff.
- **Stanley Mortensen** scored the first hat-trick, three goals in a match, when playing for Blackpool in 1953.
- **The 1970 Wembley final** between Chelsea and Leeds had to be replayed after they drew 2–2. Chelsea won the replay 2–1 at Old Trafford.

▲ *Wembley Stadium was the setting in 1923 of the first FA Cup final, when West Ham lost 0–2 to Bolton.*

Trophies

- **Football's first World Cup** was called The Jules Rimet Trophy, named after the FIFA president who organized the first competition.
- **The Calcutta Cup**, contested by England and Scotland at Rugby Union, is made from melted down rupees, the currency of India.
- **Liverpool Football Club** won the most trophies at Wembley – 17 from four different competitions: the FA Cup, the Football League Cup, the Charity Shield and the European Cup.
- **The Vince Lombardi Trophy**, made entirely of sterling silver, is presented to the winners of the Super Bowl in American football.
- **The figure on top of the Ryder Cup** is a gentleman called Abe Mitchell, a British golfer who tutored Charles Ryder on the finer points of the game.
- **British boxers** receive a Lonsdale Belt for winning three title fights in the same weight category.
- **The Stanley Cup** in ice hockey is the oldest trophy to be competed for by professional athletes in North America.

▲ *Football's World Cup is presented every four years.*

- **Axa Sun Life**, sponsors of the FA Cup, are an insurance company.
- **In the 20th century** Liverpool Football Club won the Football League Championship more times than any other team, lifting the trophy on 18 occasions.
- **Ten trophies and the sports** they are connected with: Swaythling Cup for table tennis, Air Canada Silver Broom for curling, Bologna Trophy for swimming, Sheffield Shield for cricket, Eisenhower Trophy for golf, Iroquois Cup for lacrosse, Thomas Cup for badminton, Wolfe-Noel Cup for squash, Lugano Trophy for walking, Admiral's Cup for yachting.

▶ *One of the most prestigious trophies in the tennis world is awarded to the winner of the men's singles finals.*

World champions

- **In 1986** at the age of 20, Mike Tyson became the world heavyweight champion in boxing.
- **The first world championship** in hang-gliding was held in 1975, and saw Australia winning one gold and two bronze medals.
- **In football** the World Club Cup was first contested in 1960 with Real Madrid being crowned world champions.
- **In motor racing** the oldest Formula One world champion is Juan Manuel Fangio, who won his fifth world title in 1957 at the age of 46. The youngest is Emerson Fittipaldi, who became the world champion in 1972, aged 25.
- **In 2001 Ronnie O'Sullivan** became the first Englishman since 1991 to win the World Snooker Championship, when he beat John Higgins 18–14 in the final.
- **In football** the Women's World Cup was first held in 1991 with the United States winning the tournament. In 1995 Norway were world champions; four years later the United States won the trophy for the second time; and in 2003 Germany took the title.
- **Between 1983 and 1997** Russian athlete Sergei Bubka won the first six world championships for the pole-vault. In 1985 he became the first man to clear a height of 6 m.
- **In showjumping events** the winners of the world team championship are presented with the Prince Philip Trophy. Other leading trophies with a royal connection are the Queen Elizabeth II Cup and the George V Gold Cup.

▲ *Racing-car driver Juan Manuel Fangio driving in the 1954 World Sportscar Championship.*

- **In 2001** British rider James Dobbs became world motocross champion in the 125cc class, eight years after breaking both of his arms in a crash.
- **Australia won the Cricket World Cup** in 2003 and 1999, Sri Lanka in 1996, Pakistan in 1991, Australia in 1987, India in 1983, the West Indies in 1979 and in 1975.

Table tennis

- **Fred Perry**, the famous Wimbledon champion of the 1930s, was also a world champion at table tennis.
- **A table tennis table** is 2.74 m long, 1.5 m wide, stands 0.76 m from the ground, with a net of 15.25 cm in height.
- **The player** who reaches 21 points first with at least a two-point lead, wins a game of table tennis.
- **Unlike in the game of tennis**, a volley is an illegal shot in table tennis. During a rally the ball must bounce once on the table before a player can hit it. Each player has five services in turn and a serve must bounce on each side of the net.
- **The two most popular grips** for holding the bat are called the shakehand grip, favoured by European players, and the penhold grip, favoured by Asian players.

▲ *Fred Perry won the world table tennis title in 1929 and went on to win the men's Wimbledon tennis singles in 1936.*

...FASCINATING FACT...
Table tennis was first played at the Olympic Games in Seoul in 1988.

- **The game, then known as ping-pong**, originated in the 19th century and was mainly played as an after-dinner entertainment.
- **A table tennis bat** has pimples on one side and is plain on the other. The regulations state that there should be no fewer than ten and no more than 50 pimples per square centimetre.
- **The diameter of a table tennis ball** is 40 mm and the weight is 2.7 gm. The balls are not actually hollow because they are slightly pressurized with gas.
- **Regulations laid down** by the International Table Tennis Federation state that the blade or hitting surface of a table tennis bat should contain a minimum of 85 per cent wood.

◄ *The modern table tennis bat has evolved from a long-handled racket.*

'Athlons

- **The name of the decathlon** is derived from the Greek words *dec* and *athlon* meaning 'ten' and 'contest'.
- **Daley Thompson** is the only British athlete to have won an Olympic gold medal at the decathlon, which he first achieved in 1984 with an Olympic record points total of 8847.
- **A triathlon** consists of three disciplines, a 1.5-km swim, a 40-km cycle race and a 10-km run. A sprint version of the event consists of a 0.75-km swim, 20-km cycle and a 5-km run.
- **At the 2000 Sydney Olympics** Denise Lewis, despite nursing an Achilles tendon injury, became the first British female athlete to win a heptathlon Olympic gold medal.
- **The triathlon** world championship is called the Hawaiian Ironman and was established in 1978 by a naval officer.
- **In the ancient Olympics** the pentathlon consisted of the discus, the javelin, jumping, running and wrestling.
- **The biathlon events** are rifle-shooting and skiing contests.

◀ *The javelin event is part of both the decathlon and heptathlon competitions.*

- **In the modern Olympics** the pentathlon consists of pistol-shooting, horse riding, swimming, fencing and cross-country running.
- **In a heptathlon** athletes compete in a punishing group of events – the 100-m hurdles, 200-m and 800-m running races, long jump, high jump, javelin and shot put.
- **The events in a decathlon** are even more punishing – 100-m, 400-m and 1500-m running races, 110-m hurdles, long jump, high jump, pole-vault, discus, javelin and shot put.

▲ *Sweden's Carolina Kluft clears the high jump in the women's heptathlon in the 2003 IAAF World Athletics Championships.*

Motor racing

▲ *Signalling the end of the race.*

- **The Indianapolis 500 race** is started with the words, "Ladies and gentlemen start your engines". It is contested over 200 laps, but got its name because it covers a distance of 500 miles.
- **In Formula One racing** the first six placed drivers receive championship points getting ten, six, four, three, two and one points respectively.
- **The first-ever race** in the Formula One world championship was held at Silverstone in 1950. The highest placed British driver was called Reg Parnell, who finished third despite hitting a hare during the race.
- **Here are some Formula One flags** and what they signify: blue flag – a car is about to overtake; yellow flag – danger do not overtake; black flag – a driver is disqualified; red flag – the race has ended prematurely; yellow and red flag – oil on the track; black and white chequered flag – end of race.
- **The overall width of a Formula One car** must be no greater than 180 cm and the weight must be a minimum 600 kg.
- **The first cars were built** in 1885 and it was only nine years later that the first car competition was held from Paris to Rouen and back.
- **The Monaco Grand Prix**, held in Monte Carlo, is contested over 78 laps and is the only Grand Prix race that takes place through a town's streets.

- **In 1994 Formula One world champion** Ayrton Senna was killed in a crash. The President of Brazil declared three days of national mourning and closed all schools on the day of the funeral.
- **The Grand Prix** has taken place in Buenos Aires (Argentina), Monza (Italy), Montreal (Canada), Sepang (Malaysia), Suzuka (Japan), Silverstone (Great Britain), Estoril (Portugal), Imola (San Marino), Zandvoort (Netherlands) and Budapest (Hungary).

▲ *Jacques Villeneuve powers his V-10 engined Williams to another win.*

...FASCINATING FACT...
In the world of Formula One it is forbidden for any person under the age of 16 to be allowed into the pit area.

Sporting ladies

- **Billie Jean King** was the first woman to be voted Sportsman of the Year by the editors of *Sports Illustrated.*
- **In 1926 teenager Gertrude Ederle** became the first woman to swim the English Channel.
- **Mary Queen of Scots** became the first woman to play golf at St Andrews Golf Club in Scotland, in 1522.
- **At Wimbledon 2003** the first three seeded women were: (1) Serena Williams, (2) Kim Clijsters and (3) Justin Henin-Hardenne.
- **Jamaican sprinter Merlene Ottey** has won more medals in the World Athletics Championship than any other female athlete. Her tally amounts to three gold, four silver and seven bronze medals. She also won three silver medals and five bronze medals at the Olympic Games.
- **In 1971 Princess Anne** was voted BBC Sports Personality of the Year for her high standard of showjumping.
- **When TV chef Delia Smith** became a director of Norwich City Football Club she organized for better pies to be served on the club menu after supporters claimed their half-time snacks were the worst in the land.
- **The first women's professional boxing** bout in Britain took place in 1998, when Jane Couch, 'The Fleetwood Assassin', beat Simona Lukic.
- **In athletics, the throwing competitions** that women compete in are the shot put, the javelin and the discus. The only throwing event they do not participate in is the hammer.
- **Since World War II** only three British women have won the women's singles title at Wimbledon. They are Angela Mortimer in 1961, Ann Jones in 1969 and Virginia Wade in 1977.

▲ *Billie Jean King was six times women's singles champion at Wimbledon and four times winner at the US Open.*

Sport in the sky

- **A hang-glider** powered by an engine is known as a microlite.
- **The French brothers** Etienne and Joseph Montgolfier invented the hot-air balloon. Their invention was first successfully launched in 1783, travelling 2.4 km in ten minutes and climbing to a height of 1800 m.
- **The part of a parachute** that catches the air is known as the canopy.
- **Bungee jumping** originated on the Pentecost island of Vanuatu. The jumps were performed as a ritual in an attempt to ensure a good harvest for the coming year.
- **A hot-air balloon** has three main parts. These are the burner that heats the air causing the balloon to rise, the balloon envelope that contains the air, and the basket that carries the passengers.

▲ *The Montgolfier brothers experiments stimulated further scientific interest in aviation.*

- **The first-ever recorded parachute jump** was made in the 17th century by a Hungarian called Fauste Veranzio who jumped from the top of a bell tower in Venice.
- **The world record speed** for a glider plane was set in 1997 by American James Payne who achieved an average speed of 217.41 km/h over a 100-km course.

▲ *Bungee jumping has become a very popular sport.*

- **Hang-gliding** is so called because the pilot 'hangs' beneath the wings. The glider is controlled by the pilot, who shifts his weight backwards or forwards and left or right on the control frame.
- **In 1987 Per Linstrand and Richard Branson** became the first to cross the Atlantic Ocean in a hot-air balloon.
- **The official British Army Parachute Display Team** is called The Red Devils. It was formed in 1964 and all the team members are serving soldiers in the parachute regiment.

Sporting equipment

- **The width between the goal posts** in American football is 5.6 m, in field hockey it is 3.66 m, in ice hockey it is 1.93 m, in Association Football it is 7.3 m and in Rugby Union it is 5.5 m.
- **A *coquille*** is the name of the small bell-shaped guard that fits over the fencing sword as a safety device.
- **In lacrosse** the stick is called a crosse. The attackers use a crosse with a maximum length of 1.09 m while the defenders' crosse is a maximum 1.8 m in length.
- **The football rules** state that the corner flags on the pitch must have a minimum height of 1.52 m.
- **The No. 5 iron golf club** was originally called a *mashie* and a No. 7 iron club was originally called a *mashie-niblick*.
- **The heights of hurdles** in athletics are: 1.06 m in 110-m men's race; 0.91 m in 400 m men's race; 0.83 m in 100-m women's race; and 0.76 m in 400-m women's race.

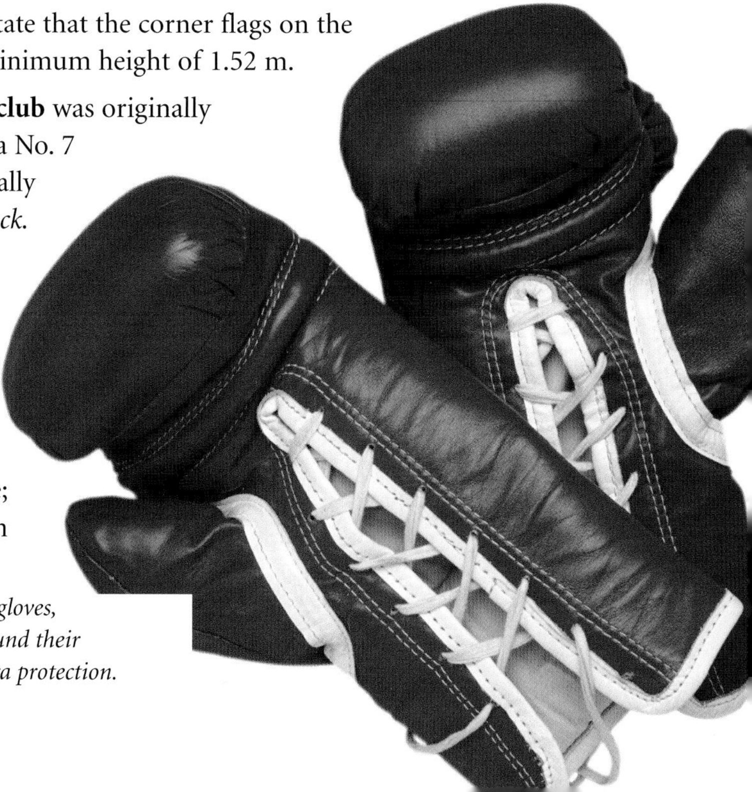

▶ *Before putting on their gloves, boxers wind bandages around their hands and thumbs for extra protection.*

- **There are six metal hoops** used on a croquet lawn, each of which stands 30 cm high. These hoops are white in colour with the crown on the first hoop painted blue and on the last hoop painted red.
- **The baton** used in athletics relay races has a maximum length of 30 cm and a circumference of 13 cm.
- **The targets in clay pigeon shooting** are neither made of clay nor are they pigeons. The targets are similar in shape to a small frisbee and are made from a mixture of lime and pitch.
- **The items a football referee** takes onto the pitch are: a whistle, a coin, a notebook, a pencil, a yellow card, a red card, a stop watch and a spare watch.

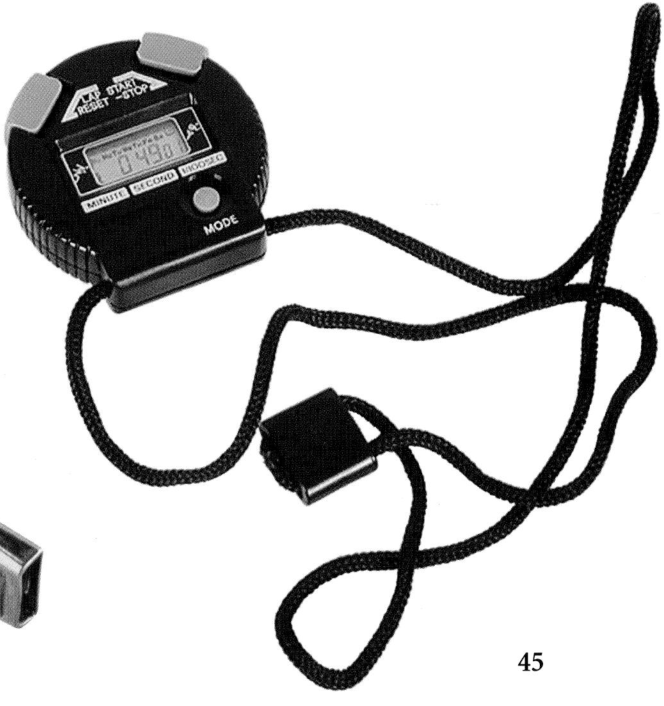

▶ *A stopwatch and whistle are vital pieces of equipment for the football referee.*

The Oxford and Cambridge boat race

- **The first Oxford and Cambridge boat race** took place in 1829 in the same year that the Cambridge University Boat Club was founded. The race was won by Oxford.
- **In 1927** the race was covered for the first time by BBC Radio and was televised for the first time by the BBC in 1938.
- **A total of 18 people** take place in the race. There are eight rowers and one cox per boat. The Cambridge reserve crew is called Goldie and the Oxford reserve crew is called Isis.
- **Since 1845** the race has been contested over a distance of 6.8 km, starting at Putney and finishing at Mortlake.
- **On average the race lasts approximately 20 minutes.** However, the record time is 16 minutes, 19 seconds set by the Cambridge crew in 1998.
- **In 1981 Sue Brown** became the first female to compete in the boat race when she coxed the Oxford crew to victory.
- **During the race** the crews pass under two bridges – Hammersmith and Barnes. Both boats must pass through the central arches of the bridges and face disqualification if they do not do so.
- **The only time a dead heat occurred** in the race was in 1877. The result, however, was shrouded in controversy, as the judge on the winning line was asleep under a bush when the race finished.
- **The Oxford and Cambridge** boat race is one of the few of the world's races rowed on tidal water.

▲ *In 1859, 1978 and 1984 the Cambridge crew sank. In 1925 and 1981 the Oxford crew sank. By an eerie coincidence in 1912, the same year the* Titanic *sank, both crews in the boat race sank.*

Animals in sport

▲ *In trotting races the drivers wear coloured silks, just as in flat racing.*

- **The racing pigeon** is the fastest animal competing in sport. It can clock up speeds of over 160 km/h.
- **Prior to the 1966 football World Cup** the trophy was mislaid and eventually found under a bush in South London by a dog called Pickles.
- **In falconry** the leather strap attached to the bird's leg is called a jess.

- **In order to make it easier to follow the race**, greyhounds wear coloured jackets according to which trap, or lane, they are running in. Trap 1 – red, Trap 2 – blue, Trap 3 – white, Trap 4 – black, Trap 5 – yellow and Trap 6 – black and white stripes.
- **In the game of darts,** hitting the bull twice in a set of three throws is known as a black dog.
- **The premier sled dog race** is called the Iditarod Trail Sled Dog Race. It is contested in the American state of Alaska over a distance of 1760 km.
- **In harness or trotting races** the jockey sits in a carriage called a sulky, which is attached to and pulled by a horse.
- **In the Aintree Grand National** the horses jump 30 fences, the highest of which stands at 1.57 m and is called The Chair.
- **Some national Rugby Union teams** have animal nicknames: Argentina (the Pumas), South Africa (the Springboks), New Zealand (the Kiwis), Australia (the Wallabies) and the United States (the Eagles).
- **Mansfield Town** is nicknamed the Stags. Other teams associated with particular animals are: Leicester City (the Foxes), Derby County (the Rams), Watford (the Hornets) and Shrewbury Town (the Shrews).

▼ *Greyhound racing is a popular spectator sport and was invented in the US in 1919.*

Chess

▼ *The pieces on a chess board are known as chessmen.*

- **The game of chess** originated in India around 100BC and was called Chaturanga.
- **In 1996, chess world champion** Gary Kasparov beat a computer specifically programmed to play chess, following a challenge issued by the IBM computer company.

- **The word 'checkmate'** is derived from the Persian term *Shah Mat,* meaning 'the King is dead'.
- **A chessboard** has 32 white squares and 32 black squares. At the start of play each player has eight pawns, two rooks, two knights, two bishops, one queen and one king.
- **In the game of chess** top-ranked players are known as Grandmasters and must achieve a score of 2400 points on the ELO ratings to attain this title. The ELO ratings were named after Dr Arpad Elo, who developed the system.
- **In the game of chess**, white always moves first. The weakest piece is a pawn. However, should a pawn manage to reach the other end of the board without being taken it can be exchanged for any other piece.
- **During World War II** the Japanese confiscated any books associated with chess because they believed that they contained secret military codes.
- **The first world chess champion** was a Czechoslovakian player called Wilhelm Steinitz, who began his reign in 1886. To date no British player has been world chess champion. The first American player to be world chess champion was Bobby Fisher from 1972 to 1975.
- **The French names** for chess pieces are *Roi* (King), *Dame* (Queen), *tour* (rook), *cavalier* (knight), *fou* (bishop) and *pion* (pawn).

...FASCINATING FACT...

There are 318, 979, 564,000 ways of playing the first four moves per side in a game of chess.

Arenas

- **The Houston Astrodome** was the first baseball stadium to have a roof over its playing field.
- **The venues for the tennis Grand Slam Tournaments**: Wimbledon (Wimbledon, London), Australian Open (Melbourne Park), US Open (Flushing Meadows, New York) and French Open (Roland Garros Stadium, Paris).
- **One of the trains** used to transport the materials for building Wembley stadium is buried beneath the stadium.
- **As of 2003** the total number of spectators that these premier football grounds could hold was as follows: Old Trafford – 68,936, Elland Road – 40,204, Goodison Park – 40,200, Anfield – 41,000, Highbury – 38,500.
- **A golf course** within 6.5 km of the coast is called a links.
- **Wembley Stadium** had 39 steps leading up to the Royal Box.
- **Some of the football clubs** that have moved to new stadiums: Stoke City – moved from the Victoria Ground to the Britannia Stadium; Derby County – moved from the Baseball Ground to Pride Park; Middlesbrough – moved from Ayresome Park to the Riverside Stadium; Huddersfield Town – moved from Leeds Road to the McAlpine Stadium; and Sunderland – moved from Roker Park to the Stadium of Light.
- **The largest football stadium** in the world is the Maracana in Rio de Janeiro, which hosted the 1950 World Cup final in front of a crowd of 199,854. Today the crowd capacity is limited to 80,000 as parts of the stadium are deemed to be unsafe.

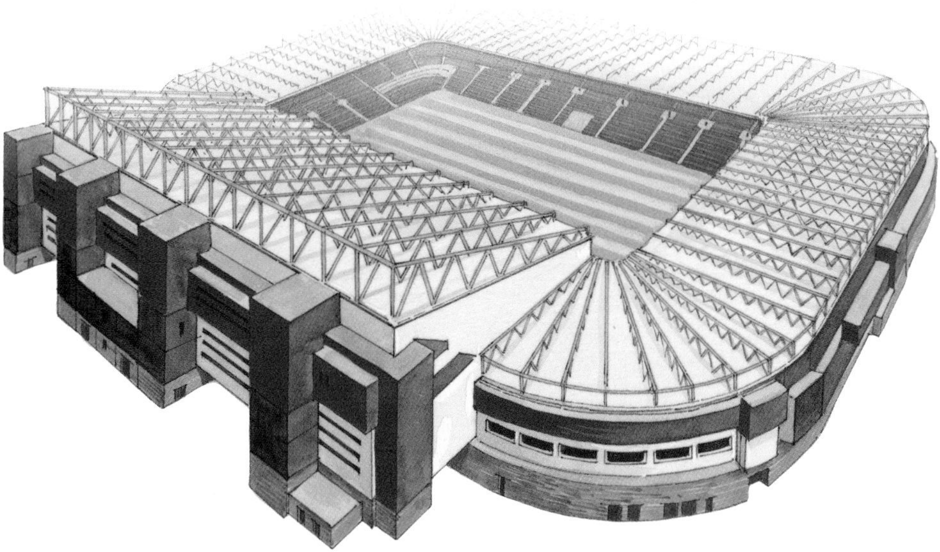

▲ *Old Trafford in Manchester is home to Manchester United Football Club.*

- **Between 1923 and 2000** 72 FA Cup finals were staged at Wembley. Various other venues have staged the final, most notably the Crystal Palace on 20 occasions and the Kennington Oval on 19 occasions.
- **Some football club home grounds**: Chelsea – Stamford Bridge, Aston Villa – Villa Park, Ipswich Town – Portman Road, West Ham – Upton Park, West Bromwich Albion – the Hawthorns, Newcastle – St James Park, Blackburn Rovers – Ewood Park, Manchester City – City of Manchester Stadium, Queen's Park Rangers – Loftus Road, Tottenham – White Hart Lane.

Baseball

- **The names of some leading baseball teams** and where they come from: Phillies (Philadelphia), Pirates (Pittsburgh), White Sox (Chicago), Red Sox (Boston), Yankees (New York), Reds (Cincinnati), Cardinals (St Louis), Dodgers (Los Angeles).
- **In professional baseball** there are nine players on each team. Each team bats for nine innings on a pitch called a diamond.
- **In 1846 Alexander Cartwright** of the Knickerbocker Baseball Club established the rules of baseball known today as the Cartwright Rules.
- **The baseball bats** used in the major league are made from ash and have a maximum length of 106.7 cm.
- **The pitcher** stands on a bar of rubber in an area known as the pitcher's mound. The rubber measures 60.96 x 15.24 cm. The distance between the pitcher and the batter is 21.05 m.
- **The most important competition** in baseball is called the World Series and is contested between the winners of the American League and the winners of the National League. The first World Series final was played in 1903 and saw the Boston Red Sox beating the Pittsburgh Pirates 5–3.
- **Four umpires** are required to officiate at a game of baseball. One is positioned at home plate and the others at the remaining three bases.

...FASCINATING FACT...

A gentleman by the name of Abner Doubleday is credited with inventing the game of baseball, and legend has it that he was also the person who fired the first shot in the US Civil War.

◀ *Until the 2000 Sydney Olympics baseball was restricted to amateurs, but now professional players are admitted.*

- **In baseball** the bases are one of the four points that must be touched by a runner in order to score a run.
- **The winners of the World Series** in 2002 were the Anaheim Angels; in 2001 the Arizona Diamondbacks; in 2000–1998 the New York Yankees; in 1997 the Florida Marlins; in 1996 the New York Yankees; in 1995 the Atlanta Braves; and in 1993 and 1992 the Toronto Blue Jays, who became the first team from outside the United States to win the World Series. In 1994 the competition was not played as the players were on strike.

Football nicknames

- **Plymouth Argyle Football Club** are nicknamed the Pilgrims because the Pilgrim Fathers sailed from Plymouth on their historic voyage to the United States of America.
- **When Manchester United** play Southampton then the Red Devils play the Saints and when Hull City play Millwall the Tigers face the Lions.

▲ *Luton Town are known as the Hatters.*

- **When Sunderland moved from Roker Park** to the Stadium of Light they changed their nickname from the Rokerites to the Black Cats.
- **Grimsby Town Football Club** are nicknamed the Mariners because the town is an important fishing port. The fans are known for waving inflatable fishes at matches.

▶ *Norwich City Football Club are known as the Canaries.*

- **Wimbledon and Aberdeen** both share the nickname of the Dons.
- **The actor Sean Bean**, who plays Sharpe on television, sports a tattoo on his arm reading '100% Blade', the nickname of his favourite team, Sheffield United.

- **The only English team** to be nicknamed after a city's building is York City. Their official nickname is the Minstermen after the cathedral of York Minster.
- **'Tasty' nicknames** of football clubs include: Everton, nicknamed the Toffeemen; Reading, known as the Biscuitmen; and Bournemouth, who are the Cherries.
- **Several British football clubs are named after birds**: Sheffield Wednesday (the Owls); Newcastle United (the Magpies); Brighton (the Seagulls); Crystal Palace (the Eagles); Norwich City (the Canaries); Bristol City (the Robins); Cardiff City (the Bluebirds); and Swansea City (the Swans).
- **Clubs named after occupations**: Walsall (the Saddlers); Luton Town (the Hatters); Northampton Town (the Cobblers); Rotherham United (the Merry Millers); and Crewe Alexandra the Railwaymen).

▶ *Bournemouth are the Cherries.*

Hockey

- **The unusual game** of octopush is hockey played under water.
- **The duration of a hockey match** is 70 minutes, divided into two periods of 35 minutes each. The match begins with a bully-off.
- **The National Hockey Stadium** of England is located in the town of Milton Keynes.
- **A hockey pitch** is 91.4 m long and 55 m wide with the goal crossbar being 2.14 m high.
- **Hockey is an 11-a-side game** and teams usually have five forwards, three halfbacks, two full backs and one goalkeeper, with five substitutes on the bench.
- **Hockey** is one of the oldest stick-and-ball games, with versions of the game dating back to the Aztec civilization of Mexico. The first official club to be established in Britain was the Blackheath Club of London, founded in 1861.
- **At the 2000 Olympics** the men's hockey gold medal was won by the Netherlands with Australia collecting the women's gold medal. The most successful Olympic team in men's hockey is India, who won a total of eight gold medals in the 20th century. Britain's men's team also won three gold medals in 1908, 1920 and 1988.
- **Hockey goalkeepers** are the only players on the pitch that are allowed to wear a hard protective helmet. The only time goalkeepers are allowed into the opponents' half of the pitch is when they are taking penalty strokes.
- **The national hockey team** of Australia are known as the Kookaburras.

- **Rules of hockey state** that the hockey stick must have a maximum weight of 737 g and the head of the stick must have a maximum length of 100 mm.

▲ *Initially, hockey was a men's game, but after World War II women's clubs took off.*

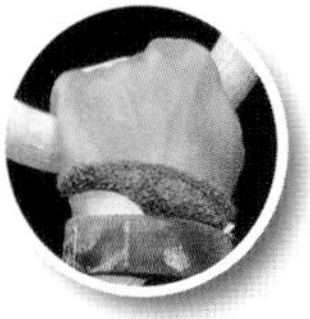

Gymnastics

- **At the age of 15**, at the 1976 Olympics, Nadia Comaneci became the first gymnast to achieve a perfect score of ten.
- **The floor exercises** in gymnastics are performed on a square mat that measures 12 x 12 m. Points are deducted by the judges even if the gymnast should put one foot outside this area
- **Soviet gymnast** Larissa Latynina won a record 18 Olympic medals between 1956 and 1964.
- **Women's rhythmic gymnastics** are performed to music using various equipment. These are a rope, a hoop, a ball, clubs and a ribbon.

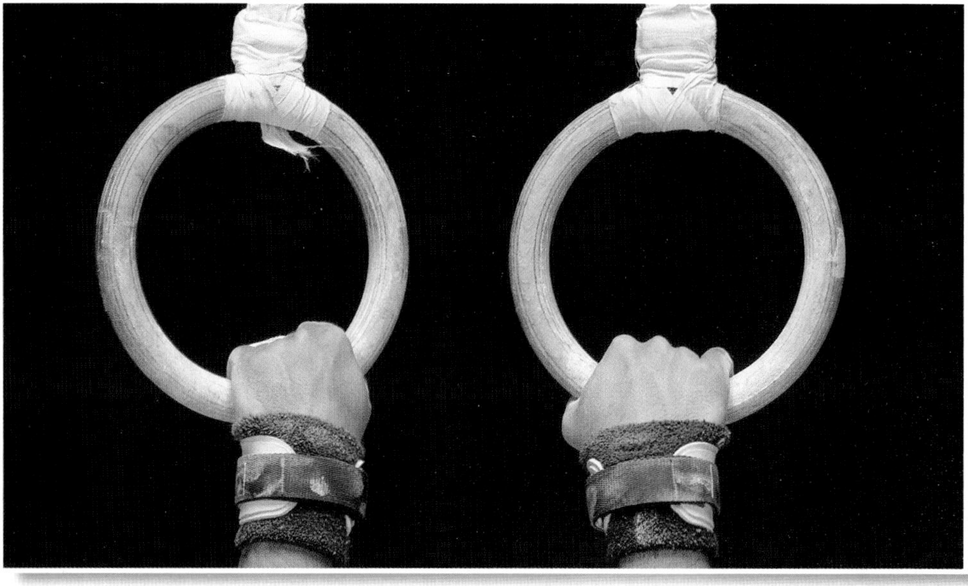

▲ *The rings are the most physically demanding piece of apparatus.*

- **In 1976 gymnast Shun Fujimoto** secured an Olympic gold medal for the Japanese men's team with his performance on the rings despite the fact that, during the previous days events, he had broken his kneecap while performing his floor routine.
- **Gymnastic events** are performed on various pieces of apparatus and each are scored by a panel of judges with a maximum mark of ten. The gymnasts are marked on their ability to demonstrate agility, timing, strength and flexibility, and the judges take into consideration the difficulty of the moves when issuing the marks.
- **The four disciplines** for women's gymnastics are floor, beam, asymmetric bars and vault.
- **The six disciplines** for men's gymnastic are floor, rings, high bar, parallel bars, vault and pommel horse.
- **The word 'gymnasium'** is derived from the Greek word *gymnos* meaning, naked.

...FASCINATING FACT...
The width of the women's balance beam is a mere 10 cm, which is 2 cm less than the diameter of a compact disc.

▶ *The combination of body strength and supplements is essential in gymnastics.*

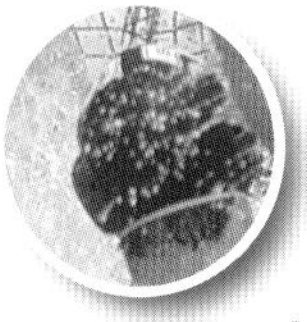

Water sports

- **In 1967 Donald Campbell** was killed on Coniston Water, Cumbria, while attempting to beat the water speed record in his vessel *Bluebird.* His body was never recovered.
- **In 1900 men's water polo** became the first team sport to be added to the Olympic programme. The women's event did not feature until the 2000 Games at Sydney.
- **In scuba diving**, scuba stands for self contained underwater breathing apparatus.
- **Water polo** is a seven-a-side sport. Goalkeepers wear a red cap to distinguish them from the other players. The game is played with a ball approximately the same size as a football and it is thrown at speeds approaching 100 km/h.
- **The manoeuvre** for correcting a capsized canoe is called an Eskimo roll. This involves turning the canoe through a complete 360° circle, 180° of which is under water.

- **The coaching staff** for synchronized swimming includes a choreographer, musical director, and makeup artist. Olympic events contain categories for solo competitors, duets and team events.

◀ *Donald Campbell in* Bluebird, *1955.*

▲ *Water polo developed in England in the middle of the 19th century.*

- **Peter Scott** son of the famous explorer Robert Falcon Scott, won a bronze medal for yachting at the 1936 Olympic Games.
- **The first official surfing championship** was held at a Sydney beach in 1964 and was won by an Australian surfer called Bernard Farrelly.
- **The four basic body positions** for divers in competition events are: free – the body position is optional, layout – the body is straight not bent, tuck – hunched body with knees together and the hands on the lower part of the legs, pike – the trunk is bent at the hips with the legs kept straight.

FASCINATING FACT

At the Mexican resort of Acapulco, cliff divers, some as young as 14, perform death-defying leaps from the La Quebrada rocks, from heights reaching 40 m.

Skiing

- **Olympic ski-jumping** is contested from two different-sized hills, 120 and 90 m high.
- **The word 'ski'** means snowshoe in the Norwegian language and the word 'luge' is derived from the French word for sled.
- **Olympic races** in men's cross-country skiing are contested over distances of 15 km, 30 km, 50 km and four 10-km stages of relay.
- **The sport of freestyle skiing** is a combination of skiing and acrobatics and consists of two disciplines called moguls and aerials. In the mogul event skiers descend down a bumpy course, and in the aerial event the skiers perform acrobatic leaps, which are marked by judges.
- **Pacific Railroad engineers** at Sun Valley ski resort in the American state of Idaho built the world's first ski chairlift.
- **In slalom and giant slalom races**, skiers travel downhill in the fastest possible time and have to zigzag through a series of gates that are marked by flags.
- **Climbing a slope** that is too steep to ski up is called herringboning. This involves striding up the hill with the skis pointing outwards in a V shape.
- **In 1980 Yuichiro Miura of Japan** became the first person to climb Mount Everest alone. Ten years earlier he also became the first person to ski down the mountain.
- **The International Ski Federation** governs official ski competitions. Their regulations state that men's skis must have a minimum length of 155 cm and a minimum width of 55 cm. Women's skis have the same minimum width and a minimum length of 150 cm.

▲ *Skiing has been well documented in history, but it only became a sport in the late 1800s.*

...FASCINATING FACT...

The 1964 Winter Olympics at Innsbruck was almost cancelled due to lack of snow. Austrian soldiers transported huge quantities of fresh snow to the Alpine venues to solve the problem.

Footballers

- **With 125 caps**, Peter Shilton is England's most-capped footballer. Pat Jennings wins that honour for Northern Ireland with 119 caps, Scotland's Kenny Daglish has 102 caps and Wales' Neville Southall has 93 caps to his name.
- **Italian footballer/manager**, Gianluca Vialli, has six toes on one foot.
- **Jack Dodds of Blackpool** scored the fastest professional hat-trick in English League Football in 1943. He scored his three goals against Tranmere Rovers in the space of two-and-a-half minutes.
- **The first-ever goal scored** in England's Premiership was bagged by Brian Deane in 1992, playing for Sheffield United against Manchester United.
- **In 2002 Michael Owen** became the sixth British player to be voted European Footballer of the Year. The previous five were Kevin Keegan (twice), George Best, Bobby Charlton, Dennis Law and Stanley Matthews.
- **Real Madrid superstar** David Beckham actually made his football league debut in Division Three, while on loan to Preston North End in the 1994–95 season
- **In April 2002 Alan Shearer** became the first player to score 200 goals in the premiership.
- **No player has yet managed to score 50 international goals** for England. To date, the nearest to achieving this feat are Bobby Charlton with 49 goals and Gary Lineker with 48 goals.
- **Current Liverpool striker** Emil Heskey has the unusual middle name of Ivanhoe. Former Liverpool star of the 90s Mark Walters has the unfortunate middle name of Everton.

▲ *Blackpool's forward Stanley Matthews, on the left, dribbles past Bolton's midfielder Barass during the English Cup final in May 1953.*

- **In 2003 Thierry Henry** was nominated as PFA Player of the Year. Other footballers to achieve this title are Ruud Van Nistelroy in 2002, Teddy Sheringham in 2001, Roy Keane in 2000, David Ginola in 1999, Dennis Bergkamp in 1998, Alan Shearer in 1997, Les Ferdinand in 1996, Alan Shearer in 1995 and Eric Cantona in 1994.

Archery

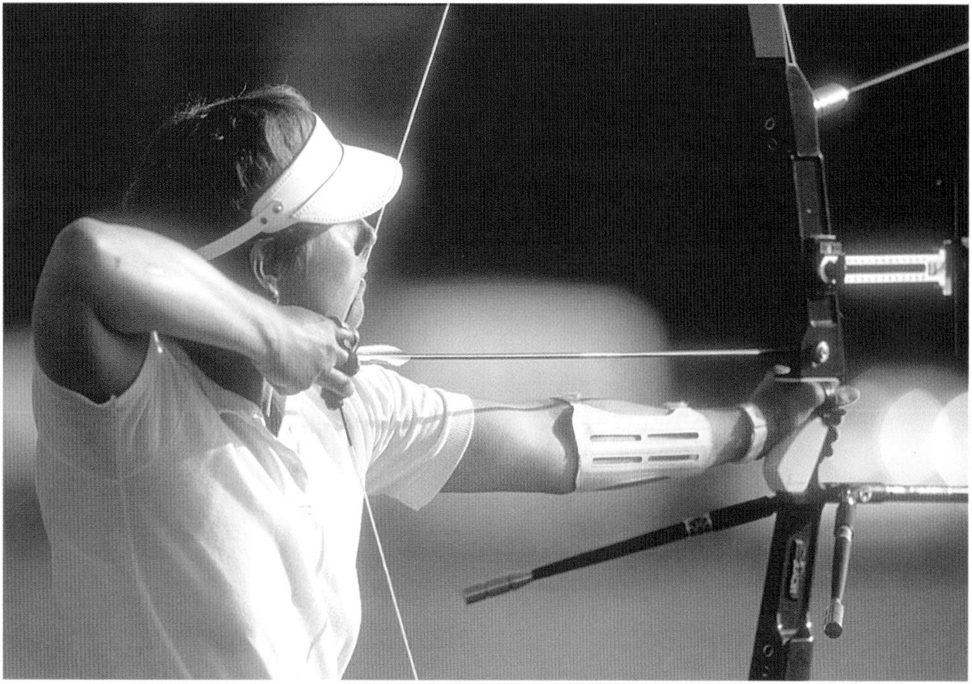

▲ *Archery is popular worldwide and was reintroduced as an Olympic event in the 1970s.*

- **One of Britain's oldest surviving** sporting contests is called the Scorton Arrow, an annual archery competition that dates back to 1637.
- **The colours of an archery target** working from the centre outwards are gold, red, blue, black and white. The gold is known as the bull's-eye and is worth ten points.

- **The art of making wooden arrows** was called fletching, but modern-day arrows are made from aluminium and carbon fibre.
- **The maximum length** permitted for a bow in the men's Olympic event is 1.82 m.
- **When an archer nocks an arrow** this means they are placing the arrow on the bowstring. The specific point where the arrow is placed is called the nocking point.
- **There are three main kinds of bow** used in archery. Longbows are traditionally made from yew. The recurve bow, used in the Olympic Games, is shorter and more powerful than the longbow. In 1966 the compound bow was developed in the United States, and comes complete with a telescopic sight.
- **The legend of Robin Hood** lives on in modern-day archery. The term given to two arrows that are shot with the second splitting the first is known as a Robin Hood.
- **Forming a Q**. The container in which an archer places his arrows is called a quiver and the bolt that is shot from a crossbow is called a quarrel.
- **Three English kings** have been killed by arrows: Richard the Lionheart in France, William Rufus in the New Forest and King Harold at the Battle of Hastings.
- **Olympic rules state** that an archery target must be 70 m away from the archer, have a diameter of 122 cm, with the centre of the bull's-eye standing 130 cm above the ground.

Trampolining

- **The sport of trampolining** did not make its Olympic debut until the Sydney 2000 Games. Alexandre Moskalenko of Russia won the first men's gold medal with a score of 41.7 out of a possible maximum score of 45. The women's gold was collected by Irina Karavaeva, also of Russia, with a score of 38.9.
- **Rules in competition trampolining** state that the height of the gym's ceiling must be at least 8 m as, on average, a trampolinist reaches heights of 6 m.
- **American George Nissen**, who invented the modern trampoline in the 1930s, built his first one in his parent's garage.
- **A Rudolph is a front somersault** with one-and-a-half twists and a Randolph is a front somersault with two-and-a-half twists.
- **On average, trampolines** measure 4.28 x 2.14 m and stand 1 m off the ground, with the bed having a thickness of 6 mm.
- **The US Air Force and NASA** both use trampolines in the training of pilots and astronauts.
- **In international competitions** a trampolinist performs ten skills. Top athletes spend around two seconds between each bounce in the air, making each routine last approximately 20 seconds.
- **In synchronized trampolining** two people have to jump on separate trampolines in time with each other performing identical routines.
- **Seven countries formed** the International Trampoline Federation in 1964. The first world championship was held at the Royal Albert Hall in London. By the end of the 20th century, 42 countries were represented in the Federation.

▲ *Trampolining is a low-impact aerobic form of exercise that strengthens the body and improves fitness.*

...FASCINATING FACT...

The word 'trampoline' derives from a 19th-century French circus acrobat called Du Trampolin who used the trapeze safety nets to perform acrobatic stunts.

Basketball

- **A basketball ring** stands 3 m from the floor and has a diameter of 45.74 cm. The diameter of the ball is 25.4 cm.
- **The Harlem Globetrotters** were founded in 1927 by Abe Saperstein and were originally called the Savoy Five.
- **If basketball players** commit six personal fouls during a game they must be substituted.
- **A professional basketball game** is divided into four quarters, each lasting 12 minutes, and is played on a court that is 28.65 m long, 15.24 m wide.
- **Real Madrid, Barcelona**, Partizan Belgrade and AEK Athens have all won European trophies at basketball.
- **Points are scored** in basketball as follows: one point for a free throw, two points for a field goal and three points for a field goal beyond the three-point line.

▲ *Basketball is one of the fastest of all team court games.*

- **A basketball player** cannot make more than two steps without passing or bouncing the ball. A violation of this rule is known as travelling.
- **Early basketballs** had laces on the outside, which caused them to bounce at unusual angles. In 1927 a ball using concealed laces was introduced.
- **The leading basketball teams** in the United Kingdom are the Manchester Giants, London Towers, Birmingham Bullets, Edinburgh Rocks and Brighton Bears.
- **The leading basketball teams** in the United States of America are the Chicago Bulls, New York Knicks, Los Angeles Lakers, Philadelphia 76ers and the Boston Celtics.

▶ *A basketball weighs between 600 and 650g.*

Sport in South America

- **Brazilian footballer Pele** amassed a career total of 1283 goals in his first-class career.
- **At the 1951 Pan American Games** the Argentinean basketball team were disqualified for having each received a gift of a motorbike prior to the tournament.
- **The largest country** in South America that has failed to appear in the final stages of football's World Cup is Venezuela.
- **The world's highest golf course**, ski run and football stadium are all situated in the South American country of Bolivia.
- **The Copa America Cup** is the international cup competition for football nations in South America. The last five winners are Colombia in 2001, Brazil in 1999 and 1997, Uruguay in 1995 and Argentina in 1993.
- **Since World War II** the most successful nation in the sport of polo has been Argentina, largely due to the fact that they have succeeded in breeding the best ponies.
- **The five South American football nations** that played in the 2002 World Cup finals were: Brazil, Uruguay, Paraguay, Argentina and Ecuador.
- **Argentinean footballing superstar** Diego Maradona played for six clubs during his professional career. These were Argentinos Juniors, Boca Juniors, Barcelona, Napoli, Sevilla and Newell's Old Boys.
- **Three Brazilian drivers** won the Formula One world championship in the 20th century: Emerson Fittipaldi, Nelson Piquet and Ayrton Senna.

- **Brazil appeared in seven World Cup finals**: 1950 Brazil v Uruguay 1–2; 1958 Brazil v Sweden 5–2; 1962 Brazil v Czechoslovakia 3–1; 1970 Brazil v Italy 4–1; 1994 Brazil v Italy 0–0 (Brazil won 3–2 on penalties); 1998 Brazil v France 0–3; 2002 Brazil v Germany 2–0.

▲ *The legendary Brazilian footballer Pele in action in 1960.*

Motorbikes

- **The Isle of Man TT Race** was first contested in 1907. The initials TT stand for Tourist Trophy.
- **The rules of speedway state** that the bike shall not be fitted with brakes or mudguards and each individual race consists of four laps of the track.
- **The Isle of Man TT** course is 60.37 km long.
- **British rider Carl Fogarty** won the 1994 and 1995 World Superbikes Championship riding a Ducati motorbike.
- **The World Superbikes Championship** of 2002 consisted of 13 events spread across the world. Two of the races were staged in England, one at the Silverstone circuit and the other at Brands Hatch.
- **In 1974 legendary stunt rider** Evel Knievel attempted a motorcycle jump across the Snake River Canyon. His attempt was unsuccessful but remarkably he lived to tell the tale.
- **When the Isle of Man TT Race** was first contested, the winners achieved average speeds of just over 60 km/h. Today the winning riders reach speeds of over 192 km/h.
- **In 1965 West Ham** were the first winners of the British League in the sport of speedway.
- **The English military hero** Lawrence of Arabia died in 1935 in a motorcycle accident. Legend has it that his ghost can now be heard riding his motorbike near the house in Dorset where the accident occurred.
- **Seven different motorbike manufacturers** entered the 2003 World Superbikes Championship. These were Ducati, Honda, Aprilia, Kawasaki, Petronas, Yamaha and Suzuki. Just three companies, namely Dunlop, Michelin and Pirelli, supplied the tyres for these bikes.

▲ *Motorcyclists crouch low reducing drag and increasing speed.*

The Highland Games

- **Throwing events** in the Highland Games include the shot, the hammer, the caber and sheaf-tossing. The latter involves the throwing of a heavy bag of hay over a bar using a pitchfork.
- **Until 1975 when the Sex Discrimination Act** was passed, female bagpipers were not allowed to compete against men in Scotland's Highland Games.
- **The most prestigious of the games** is the Braemar Games held annually on the first Saturday in September, and attended by members of the royal family. The patron of the games is Queen Elizabeth II.

▲ *Competing in the hammer event at the Highland Games.*

- **In 1900 the Braemar Games** were cancelled at the request of Queen Victoria as a show of respect for the soldiers who had died in the Boer War. The following year they were cancelled again as a sign of respect for Queen Victoria, who died in 1901.
- **The word 'caber'** is derived from the Gaelic word for tree.

- **The Highland Games** had their beginning in Scotland but are also regularly held in the United States and Canada. At these Games, the national anthems of Scotland, Canada and the United States are all played.
- **Children's events in Scotland's Braemar Games** include sack-racing, sprints, sword-dancing and Highland flings.
- **The origins of the Braemar Games** date back to the 10th century when King Malcolm offered a prize to the clansman who won a race up and down a hill situated behind Braemar Castle.
- **An event purely for women** in the Highland Games is throwing the rolling pin, which weighs just over 11 kg and is thrown underhand with one hand only. Events for canine competitors include sheep-herding and duck-herding.

▲ *A contestant in the Strong Man competition.*

. . . FASCINATING FACT . . .

Tossing the caber is not a distance event. The object is to make the caber land pointing at the sky.

Cricketers

- **Alan Border** played in 156 Test matches for Australia and, by strange coincidence, took 156 catches in the field.
- **The first cricketer** to amass 10,000 Test runs was Sunil Gavaskar of India.
- **Batsmen are given out** if they do not appear on the field within two minutes of the previous batsman getting out. This dismissal is known as timed out.
- **In the 1988 Test Series** against the West Indies, four different players captained England, but they still lost the Series 4–0. The four were Graham Gooch, Chris Cowdrey, John Embury and Mike Gatting.
- **Former England cricket captain** Ian Botham also played League Football for Scunthorpe United, and Gary Lineker, before signing terms for Leicester City Football Club, had a chance to play for Leicestershire County Cricket Club.
- **There are three types of bowlers in cricket**. Fast bowlers can deliver the ball at speeds of up to 160 km/h while medium-paced bowlers deliver the ball at speeds of up to 100 km/h. Spin bowlers bowl a slower ball but spin it in order to deceive the batsman.
- **The five English cricketers** who scored the most Test runs in the 20th century are Graham Gooch – 8900 runs, David Gower – 8231 runs, Geoffrey Boycott – 8114 runs, Michael Atherton – 7728 runs, and Colin Cowdrey – 7624 runs.
- **At the end of the 20th century** *Wisden Almanac* listed the five greatest cricketers, as voted by leading sports writers. In order they are Sir Donald Bradman, Sir Garfield Sobers, Sir Jack Hobbs, Shane Warne and Sir Viv Richards.

- **In order to complete one run** a batsman must cover a distance of at least 17.68 m between the two creases.

▲ *West Indian captain Brian Lara cuts Kaushal Lokuarachchi during his century in a game against Sri Lanka in 2003.*

...FASCINATING FACT...

Former England cricket captain CB Fry also played football for England in the early 20th century, equalled the world long jump record and was offered the throne of Albania.

Sporting firsts

- **In 1931 tennis star** Lili de Alvarez became the first-ever woman to don a pair of shorts at Wimbledon.
- **Only 13 nations** contested the first football World Cup in 1930, which saw Uruguay winning the trophy.
- **The first ever-footballer** to win 100 caps for England was the Wolves defender Billy Wright. The only other players to have emulated this feat are Bobby Moore, Bobby Charlton and Peter Shilton.
- **Roger Bannister** ran the first under four-minute mile in 1954 at an Oxford running track: the time was 3 minutes, 59.4 seconds.
- **The first foreign footballing nation** to defeat England at Wembley was Hungary. It outplayed England in 1953, winning the game by a comfortable margin of 6–3.
- **Years in which tennis Grand Slam tournaments** were first contested: Wimbledon tournament was established in 1877, the US Open in 1881, the French Open in 1891 and the Australian Open in 1905.
- **The first winners of the major football cup competitions**: (1) FA Cup Final in 1872 was won by Wanderers; (2) European Cup Final in 1956 was won by Real Madrid; (3) Scottish Cup Final in 1874 was won by Queens Park; (4) European Nations Champions Cup in 1960 was won by the Soviet Union; (5) European Cup Winners Cup in 1961 was won by Fiorentina.

. . . FASCINATING FACT . . .

In 1504 James IV of Scotland became the first-ever king to play a game of golf.

- **In 1975 Junko Tabei** of Japan became the first woman to reach the top of Mount Everest.
- **The first English Football League team** to install an artificial pitch were Queens Park Rangers in 1981.

▶ *Junko Tabei of Japan on her ascent of Mount Everest in 1975.*

Boxing

- **The sport of boxing** did not become a legal sport until 1901. It is governed by the Queensberry Rules established by Sir John Sholto Douglas, the 8th Marquess of Queensberry. Britain's first boxing club was called the Pugilistic Club and was founded in London in 1814.
- **World championship bouts** in professional boxing are now fought over 12 three-minute rounds, with a one-minute break between each.
- **In Olympic boxing** contests the wearing of headguards is mandatory – these bouts are contested over three rounds.
- **Professional boxing rings** are enclosed by four ropes, which must have a minimum diameter of 2.54 cm. The minimum size of a ring in professional boxing is 5.48 sq m with a maximum size of 7.31 sq m.
- **The boxer Chris Eubank** was the first person to be voted out in the first-ever celebrity edition of the TV game show *Big Brother.*
- **If a boxer's trainer** believes his fighter is taking too much punishment they can throw the towel into the ring and the fight is stopped. The term 'throwing in the towel' is now commonly used to mean giving up.
- **The four controlling bodies** in professional boxing are: World Boxing Association (WBA), World Boxing Council (WBC), World Boxing Organization (WBO), International Boxing Federation (IBF).
- **Only three fighters representing Britain** have become world heavyweight champions. Bob Fitzsimmons won the title in the late 19th-century, Frank Bruno won the WBC title in 1995 and Lennox Lewis won his first world title in 1992. At the 1988 Seoul Olympics Lennox Lewis won a boxing gold medal representing Canada's national team.

- **The term** 'to throw one's hat in the ring' meaning to make a challenge derives from boxing. A boxer issuing a challenge to another boxer would literally throw his hat into the ring.
- **Maximum weight limits** for fighters in professional boxing are: flyweight 51 kg, bantamweight 54 kg, featherweight 61 kg, welterweight 67 kg, middleweight 73 kg, heavyweight boxers must weigh over 86 kg.

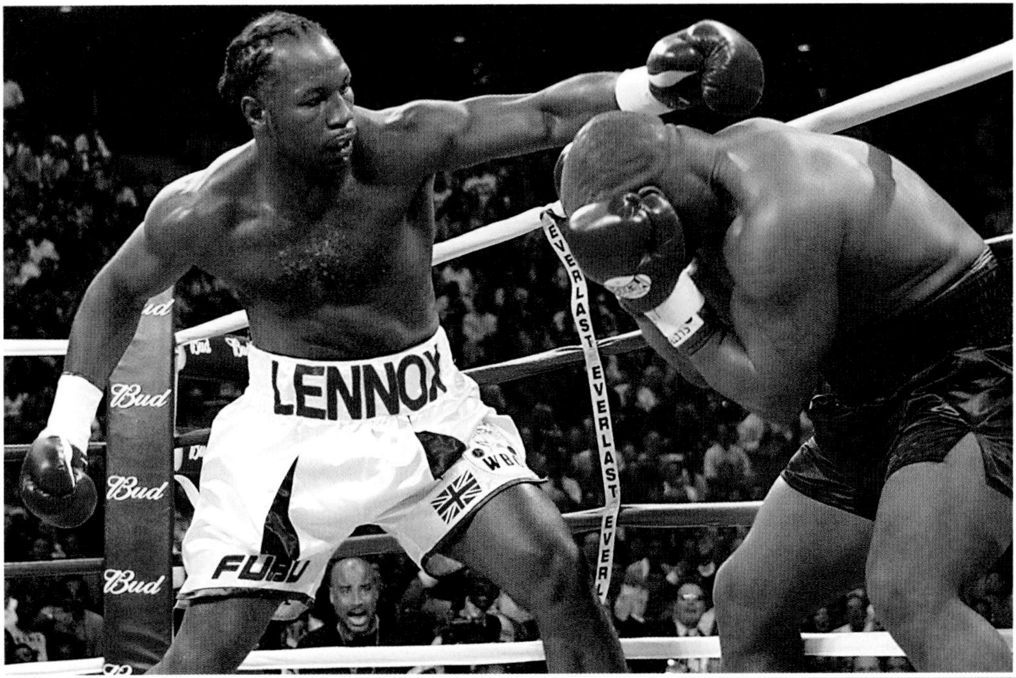

▲ *Two great heavyweights, Lennox Lewis (left) and Mike Tyson, meet in a bout in 2002.*

Football World Cup

- **When Brazil won the World Cup trophy** for the third time in 1970 they were allowed to keep the trophy permanently. When winning the World Cup for the fourth time in 1994, they were the first to win the trophy on a penalty shoot-out.
- **The only English player** to be the leading scorer in the World Cup finals was Gary Lineker, who scored six goals at the 1986 finals.
- **1958 was the only year** in which England, Scotland, Northern Ireland and Wales all qualified for the final stages of the World Cup.
- **Thirty-two nations qualified for the finals** of the 2002 World Cup, with representatives from every continent in the world. The most represented continent is Europe, with 15 nations qualifying.
- **The youngest player to win a World Cup winners medal** is Pele, at the age of seventeen in 1958. The oldest is Dino Zoff, the Italian goalkeeper, who won his medal in 1982 at the age of 40.
- **England's World Cup hero Geoff Hurst** is the only player to score a hat-trick in a World Cup final when his three goals helped England beat West Germany 4–2. The other scorer for England in that final was his West Ham teammate Martin Peters.
- **The official emblems of the 2002 World Cup** were three computer-generated characters called Nik, Kaz and Ato.
- **The original World Cup trophy**, called the Jules Rimet Trophy, was 30 cm high, made of pure gold and weighed 1.82 kg. The FIFA World Cup replaced it in 1971 and is 36 cm tall, is made of 18 carat gold and weighs 5 kg.

- **The 2002 World Cup** was the first to be played on the Asian continent and also the first to be contested in two different countries, with 32 matches being played in Japan and 32 matches in South Korea.
- **World Cup winners:**

2002 – Brazil
1998 – France
1994 – Brazil
1990 – West Germany
1986 – Argentina
1982 – Italy
1978 – Argentina
1974 – West Germany
1970 – Brazil
1966 – England
1962 – Brazil

▲ *England's David Beckham and Brazil's Ronaldo playing in the England–Brazil quarterfinal match of the FIFA 2002 Football World Cup.*

Jumping

- **High jumpers and pole-vaulters** are allowed three attempts to clear each separate height.
- **A skater called Dick Button** performed the first-ever triple jump in a skating tournament held in 1952.
- **In 1991 Mike Powell** broke Bob Beamon's 23-year-old long jump record with a jump measuring 8.95 m.
- **The poles used in pole-vaulting** competitions are on average 4 to 5 m long and weigh approximately 3.6 kg.
- **The high jump method** of jumping head first and landing on the back is called The Fosbury Flop. It was named after the American athlete Dick Fosbury, who introduced this style at the 1968 Olympic Games.
- **In the Olympics** the run-up for a pole-vaulter must be at least 40 m long, and the box in which a vaulter lodges his pole must be 1 m long and 20 cm deep.
- **In long jump and triple jump events**, the competitors must jump from or behind a 20-cm wide foul line, which is made of white plasticine. If a toe crosses the foul line a no jump, signalled by a red flag, is declared by the judges.
- **In high jump Olympic events**, the height of the bar is raised by at least 2 cm after each round. In the pole-vault the height of the bar is raised by at least 5 cm.
- **The showjumping and equestrian events** at the 1956 Melbourne Olympics could not be held in Australia due to their strict animal quarantine laws. The events were rescheduled and held five months earlier in Stockholm, Sweden.

▼ *There is a fan-shaped run-up area before the crossbar in the high jump and a cushioned landing mat beyond.*

...FASCINATING FACT...
On average, ski-jumpers jump the length of two football pitches.

Netball

- **In netball**, players are not allowed to hold the ball for more than three seconds, nor can they take more than two steps with the ball.
- **The first netball championship** was held in England in 1963 and was won by Australia. The Australian women have dominated the world championships, winning eight between 1963 and 1999.
- **A netball court** is 30.48 m long and 15.24 m wide and is divided into three equal parts.
- **Netball is a seven-a-side game** and the match is divided into four periods, each lasting 15 minutes.
- **The ball used in netball** has a circumference of 69 to 71 cm and weighs between 400 and 450 g.
- **The game of netball was invented in 1891** by a Canadian called James Naismith, who adapted the rules of basketball for a female version of the game.
- **Two umpires,** each of whom controls one half of the court from the sidelines, adjudicate the game of netball.
- **The goal post hoop** stands just over 3 m high with a diameter of 38 cm.
- **England's international netball star** Tracey Neville is the sister of Manchester United's football stars Gary and Phil Neville.
- **Initials on netball bibs** and the positions they represent are: GK – Goal Keeper, GA – Goal Attack, GD – Goal Defence, GS – Goal Shooter, WD – Wing Defence, WA – Wing Attack, C – Centre.

▲ *Netball is a non-contact sport. Much skill is needed in making passes and openings.*

Shooting

- **The national shooting centre** for Britain is the Bisley Camp, which is located in the county of Surrey.
- **William Frederick Cody**, better known as Buffalo Bill, established his own Wild West shooting show that toured the world to great acclaim. Annie Oakley, nicknamed Little Miss Sureshot, also toured with the show.
- **Samuel Colt** is credited with the invention of the revolver.
- **In the English city of York** an ancient law states that it is legal to shoot a Scotsman with a bow and arrow after sunset.
- **Shooting was included** in the first modern Olympics in 1896. In the 2000 Sydney Olympics there were 17 shooting events in total, ten for men and seven for women.
- **The UK Rifle Association** was founded in 1860 and members competed for the Sovereign's Prize, a trophy established by Queen Victoria.
- **There are three different types of target** used in Olympic competitions. These are clay, electronic and paper.
- **In air rifle shooting events** at the Olympics, competitors stand 10 m from the target, which has a bull's eye measuring just 0.5 mm in diameter.
- **In 1916 Pennsylvanian gunsmith Jones Wister** invented a rifle that had a curved barrel, which enabled it to shoot round corners.
- **The targets in clay pigeon shooting** are released from machines called traps, which eject the targets at speeds of up to 80 km/h.

▲ *US sharpshooter Annie Oakley astounded audiences in the Buffalo Bill's Wild West Show.*

Ball sports

- **The distance between** the two sets of cricket wickets is known as a chain, which is equivalent to 20.1 m.
- **Gary Player** was the only golfer in the 20th century to win the British Open in three different decades.
- **In football**, players cannot be offside in their own half or when receiving the ball direct from a throw in.
- **In hurling**, one point is awarded if the ball passes over the bar and three points awarded for under the bar.

▲ *In beach volleyball the ball must be cleanly hit or 'pop' off the hand. Opponents have to switch sides after a set number of points to equalize the advantages of sun and wind.*

- **Seven English Football League teams** have a last name beginning with A. They are Charlton Athletic, Oldham Athletic, Wigan Athletic, Crewe Alexandra, Plymouth Argyle, West Bromwich Albion and Brighton and Hove Albion.
- **In 1996 teenager Martina Hingis** became the youngest player to win a Wimbledon title, when at the age of 15 she won the women's doubles title with Helena Sukova.
- **Countries that have hosted football's World Cup** are Japan and South Korea in 2002, France in 1998, United States in 1994, Italy in 1990, Mexico in 1986, Spain in 1982, Argentina in 1978, West Germany in 1974, Mexico in 1970, England in 1966, Chile in 1962.
- **The game of volleyball** was originally called mintonette and was invented in 1895 by William George Morgan of the United States.
- **The game of korfball** originated in Holland in 1903. The word *korf* is Dutch for basket and the game is similar to basketball. The players shoot the ball with two hands through a basket that stands 3.5 m high. Teams have eight players, four men and four women.
- **In golf, a bunker is a hazard** usually filled with sand, a fairway is the playing area of a hole between the green and the tee and the 19th hole is the clubhouse bar!

Speed

- **The world's fastest ball sport** is jai alai, which is played with a ball called a pelota, which can reach speeds of over 280 km/h.
- **In September 1994** Californian Chad Hundeby set a new world record for swimming the English Channel with a time of 7 hours, 17 minutes.
- **In 2002 in Paris**, sprinter Tim Montgomery broke the world 100 m record with a time of 9.78 seconds.
- **In speedskating races** the skaters wear coloured armbands to represent their starting lanes. The skater wearing a red band starts in the outer lane and the skater starting in the inner lane wears a white band.
- **In a ten-second sprint**, humans reach an average speed of around 40 km/h. By comparison, the fastest land animal, the cheetah, attains speeds approaching 110 km/h over short distances.
- **The first-ever Grand Prix** in 1981 was won with an average speed of around 73.5 km/h. Today the top drivers exceed speeds of around 300 km/h.
- **The fastest recorded tennis serve** in the 20th century was delivered by Greg Rusedski and was timed at 239.8 km/h. Venus Williams clocked the fastest serve recorded by a woman at 205 km/h.
- **In the winter sport of skeleton racing** the competitors reach speeds of 136 km/h on a sled that has no brakes and no form of steering.
- **The average speed of a greyhound is 70 km/h**, while racehorses reach a top speed of around 49 km/h. Although a greyhound would win a race over a short distance, a horse would win races over a longer distance due to its greater stamina.

- **On October 15, 1997** Andy Green set a new land speed record of 1226.5 km/h in a car called *Thrust SSC*.

▲ Thrust SSC *is the result of over 2½ years of research into the shape of a supersonic vehicle.*

The marathon

▲ *Athletes run past the Arc de Triomphe in Paris during the men's marathon at the 9th IAAF World Athletics Championships in 2003.*

- **The world's oldest marathon** is held in Boston and was first contested in 1897. In that race, only 15 runners competed.
- **The marathon is one of the few races** that is not measured in metric distances. It is run over 26.2 miles that converts to 41.92 km.
- **At the 1960 and 1964 Olympic Games** Ethiopian runner Abebe Bikili won the gold medal for the marathon running in his bare feet.

- **The name of the marathon** derives from ancient Greece. In 490BC a soldier called Phedippides ran to Athens to tell of a victory at Marathon. He died shortly after delivering the news.
- **In 1908 at the London Olympics** an extra 352 m was added to the distance of the marathon, so that the finishing line was opposite the royal box occupied by King Edward VII.
- **British athlete Paula Radcliffe** won the 2003 women's race in the London Marathon for the second year in a row. Ethiopian athlete Gezahegne Abera won the men's race in a time of 2 hours, 7 minutes, 56 seconds.
- **In 2002, Tanni Grey-Thompson** won her sixth London Marathon in the wheelchair race, three months after giving birth to her daughter Carys.
- **When a marathon runner** reaches the point of exhaustion this is known as 'hitting the wall'. Blisters and cramp are the most common ailments affecting marathon runners.
- **The London Marathon** has been contested since 1981 and celebrity runners who have entered the race include TV gardener Charlie Dimmock, DJ Jimmy Saville, football manager John Gregory, rower Steve Redgrave, boxer Frank Bruno and sports presenter Steve Ryder.

...FASCINATING FACT...

When running a marathon it is estimated that the competitors lose, on average, 1 cm in height, due to the constant pounding that causes the body's muscles to compress.

Sporting superstars

- **The real first name** of the golfer Tiger Woods is Eldrick.
- **Boxers Muhammad Ali**, Sugar Ray Leonard and Lennox Lewis all won Olympic gold medals before becoming professional world champions.
- **Footballers who have recorded hit records** include Paul Gascoigne, Glenn Hoddle, Chris Waddle, Ian Wright and Kevin Keegan who once had a No. 1 hit in Germany.
- **Britain's richest young sportsmen** in 2003 were: David Beckham (worth £50 million), Naseem Hamed (£25 million), Michael Owen (£18 million), Sol Campbell (£15 million) and Dario Franchitti and Ryan Giggs (each worth £14 million).
- **Michael Jordan**, considered to be the greatest-ever basketball player, lead the Chicago Bulls to four NBA (National Basketball Association) titles and also played professional baseball for the Birmingham Barons.
- **In 1990, at the age of 19**, Pete Sampras became the youngest player to win the men's singles at the US Open. By the time he retired in 2003, he had won a further four US Open titles, two Australian Opens and seven Wimbledon titles.
- **The FIFA Player of the Year award** began in 1991, when Lothar Mattheus won it. Since then Marco Van Basten won it in 1992, Roberto Baggio in 1993, Romario in 1994, George Weah in 1995, Ronaldo in 1996, 1997 and 2002, Zinedine Zidane in 1998, 2000 and 2003, Rivaldo in 1999, Luis Figo in 2001.
- **Snooker star Ronnie O'Sullivan** is nicknamed The Rocket due to the speed in which he builds his breaks. In 1997 he made the fastest-ever maximum 147 break in a remarkable time of 5 minutes, 20 seconds.

- **Argentinean football star** Diego Maradona has a tattoo of the Cuban leader Fidel Castro on his left shin.

- **Boxers often fight** under a variety of nicknames. These include Iron Mike for Mike Tyson, the Prince for Naseem Hamed and the Real Deal for Evander Holyfield. the Rocky films continued the nickname theme with Rocky Balboa (the Italian Stallion) fighting Apollo Creed (the Count of Monte Fisto).

◀ *Muhammad Ali is probably the best-known athlete in the world.*

Polo

- **Polo is a four-a-side sport** and is played on the largest pitch of any team sport. The maximum dimensions of the pitch are 274.3 m long and 182.8 m wide, with goalposts that are 7.31 m wide.
- **The rules of polo state** that the game cannot be played left-handed.
- **The game of polo originated** in Persia more than 2000 years ago.
- **Polo is divided into** periods of play called chukkas, each of which lasts 7.5 minutes.
- **Polo is the favourite sport** of Prince Charles and, on occasions he has played on the same side as his sons William and Harry.
- **In the 19th century height restrictions** were placed on the ponies. The maximum height allowed for a pony was 13 hands (1.4 m) but this rule was eventually removed as the riders' legs used to drag across the ground.
- **Polo balls are made from** high-impact plastic and have a diameter between 7.62 and 8.89 cm with a weight between 120 and 135 g.
- **The sport of water polo** originated in England in the 1860s and was originally called soccer in water.
- **In the 19th century Captain John Watson**, a member of the British Cavalry 13th Hussars, was responsible for creating the first set of written rules for polo.

...FASCINATING FACT...

Polo was a favourite pastime of the royal family of China and a polo stick is depicted on the royal coat of arms of China.

▲ *Polo demands much skill and stamina of the rider and his horse or 'pony'.*

Judo

◀ *In judo, bouts usually last five minutes, though in major championships seven minutes are allowed.*

FASCINATING FACT

The word 'judo' literally means gentle way.

- **Judo for men** was first introduced into the Olympic Games in 1964 at the request of the host nation Japan, while the women's event had to wait until 1992 before making its Olympic debut.
- **The sport of judo** was derived from a form of jujitsu and was founded in 1882 by a doctor called Jigoro Kano.
- **Participants in judo** are awarded coloured belts that indicate their level of achievement. Beginners wear white, followed by yellow, orange, green, blue, brown, black and red.
- **A judo bout is fought** on a mat called a tatami and the bout commences when the referee says *hajime,* meaning begin.
- **Judo was first officially taught** in Japan at a Tokyo school called the Kodokan Judo Institute in 1882.
- **The three main techniques** used in judo are throwing techniques called *nage waza,* striking techniques called *atemi waza* and grappling techniques called *katame waza.*
- **In a judo competition** an ippon is worth one point. An ippon occurs when a contestant is thrown on their back or kept in a hold for 25 seconds. A waza-ari (worth half a point) is awarded for a less successful throw or when an opponent is held for 20 seconds.
- **A defeated opponent** unable to escape from a hold taps the floor as a sign of submission, and the attacker must release the hold immediately.
- **In judo** an *eri* is the collar on a judo costume, a *dojo* is the school or hall for learning judo, a *kyo* is a student and a *kyoshi* is the judo instructor.

Sport in Australia

- **Melbourne was the first city** in the Southern Hemisphere to host the Summer Olympics. In 2000 Sydney became the second.
- **The game of Australian Rule Football** has teams of 18 players with the substitute known as the 19th man.
- **Sydney Opera House** in Australia has the nickname 'Nine nuns in a scrum'.
- **Two of the mascots** of the 2000 Sydney Olympics were a kookaburra called Olly and a platypus called Sid.
- **In 1898, Australian swimmer Alick Wickham** introduced the crawl swimming stroke to the western world and went on to become the Australian freestyle champion.
- **The Australian national soccer team** are nicknamed the Socceroos and for a spell were managed by former England boss Terry Venables.
- **The first-ever Test match** between England and Australia took place at the Melbourne Cricket Ground in 1877. Australia won the match by 45 runs.
- **Australian Rugby Union star** David Campese scored more international tries than any other player in the history of Rugby Union, scoring 64 tries in his 15-year international career.
- **The Commonwealth Games** was hosted three times by Australia in the 20th century. The city of Sydney hosted the Games in 1938, Perth in 1962 and Brisbane in 1982.
- **The winners of the Australian Open** in tennis are: men's singles 2003 – Andre Agassi, 2002 –Thomas Johansson, 2001 – Andre Agassi, 2000 – Andre Agassi, 1999 – Yevgeny Kafelnikov, 1998 – Petr Korda; women's singles 2003 – Serena Williams, 2002 – Jennifer Capriati, 2001 – Jennifer Capriati, 2000 – Lindsay Davenport, 1999 – Martina Hingis, 1998 – Martina Hingis.

▲ *The shape of yacht sails is echoed in the archictecture of the Sydney Opera House.*

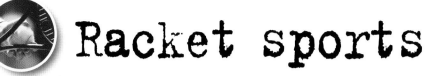

Racket sports

▲ *Wimbledon is the only Grand Slam that still has a predominantly white clothing rule.*

- **The game of squash** originated in the 19th century at Harrow School.
- **The lines on a squash court** must be 50 mm in width and coloured red.
- **Indian tennis star Vijay Amritraj** played an assistant to James Bond in the 1983 film *Octopussy*.
- **A tennis racket** must be no longer than 74.9 cm, with a hitting surface no longer than 39.37 cm and no wider than 29.2 cm.
- **Of the 32 seeded players** in the 2003 men's singles at Wimbledon, the only British representative was Tim Henman, who was seeded No. 10.

- **In the game of real tennis** the ball was originally hit with the hand, then with a gloved hand, and finally a racket was developed. In 1625 Charles I built a real tennis court at Hampton Court Palace that is still used in competitions today.

- **The game of short tennis** was developed as a mini version of lawn tennis and is played on a smaller court with smaller rackets, lower nets and spongy balls

- **The game of racquetball**, a combination of squash and handball, was developed in the United States in 1949 by Joe Sobek, a tennis professional from Connecticut, USA.

▲ *Finalists in the 14th Asian Games in the 2002 women's squash event.*

- **International tennis tournaments** are played on three different types of surfaces. They are grass courts, hard courts and clay courts.

- **The balls used in a game of squash** are marked with coloured dots to indicate their speed. A yellow clot is superslow, a white or green dot is slow, a red dot is medium fast and a blue dot is fast.

Football matches

- **In 1885 Arbroath beat Bon Accord** 36–0 in a Scottish Cup tie, which is still a British record for a game involving a League team.
- **In March 2002** the game between Sheffield United and West Bromwich Albion was abandoned after Sheffield's team were reduced to six men following sendings off and injuries.
- **In 2001 Australia** set a new record score for a World Cup match when they beat American Samoa in the qualifying rounds. The scoring was so prolific that the referee lost count not knowing whether the score was 31–0 or 32–0.
- **At the 1998 World Cup** the golden goal rule was introduced. This stated that when a match was level at the end of 90 minutes the first team to score in extra time won the match. The first match to be won using this ruling came when France beat Paraguay 1–0, with Laurent Blanc scoring the golden goal.
- **The Manchester United defenders** Gary and Phil Neville became the first brothers to play on the same England team since Bobby and Jackie Charlton in the 1960s.
- **A recent addition** to the rules of football states that 30 seconds should be added to the time of a match for every goal scored and every player substituted.
- **In 1994 the United States** played Switzerland at the Pontiac Silverdome in Detroit in the first-ever World Cup match played indoors. The match finished in a 1–1 draw.
- **England's matches in the 1966 World Cup**: Group Matches: England v Uruguay 0–0, England v Mexico 2–0, England v France 2–0; Quarterfinal: England v Argentina 1–0; Semi-final: England v Portugal 2–1; Final: England v West Germany 4–2.

- **UEFA regulations** state that a football pitch should have a length of between 90 and 120 m and a width of between 45 and 90 m.

▲ *Football is the most popular sport in the world.*

...FASCINATING FACT...

At the 1990 World Cup the players representing the United Arab Emirates international team each received a Rolls-Royce car for every goal scored by the team. By the end of the tournament they had managed to score two goals.

Cricket

▲ *Australian captain Steve Waugh holds the trophy after Australia retains the Ashes in 2003.*

- **A cricket ball** is held together by between 65 and 70 stitches.
- **The word 'cricket'** is derived from the French word *criquet*, meaning goalpost.
- **The first Test match** in England took place at the Oval in 1880 when England played Australia.
- **The Ashes Trophy** is only 10.16 cm tall. Regardless of whether Australia or England win the contest, it stays at Lord's Cricket Ground.
- **Test matches** are currently held at Headingley, Kennington Oval, Edgbaston, Lord's, Trent Bridge and Old Trafford.
- **In the game of cricket** a score of 111 is known as a Nelson and is considered by English cricketers to be an unlucky score. The name derives from Admiral Nelson whose wounds received in battle reduced him to one arm and one eye.
- **The most runs** that can be scored off one ball is eight, coming from four runs and four overthrows.

▲ *Cricket is a subtle and complicated game with eccentric names for fielding positions.*

- **Cricket Test matches** are played over a five-day period. Weather permitting, a minimum of 90 overs are bowled on each of the first four days, and a minimum of 75 overs are bowled on the last day's play.
- **In 1992 a third umpire** was introduced into the game to make decisions on television replays.
- **Many county cricket teams** in the National League have nicknames, such as Lancashire Lightning, Essex Eagles, Warwickshire Bears, Gloucestershire Gladiators and Susses Sharks.

Swimming

▲ *Male and female swimmers often favour wearing a swimming hat as it reduces the water resistance created even by short hair.*

- **The backstroke event** is the only swimming race in which the swimmers start in the water.
- **An olympic-size swimming pool** is 50 m long and has eight swimming lanes.

- **Johnny Weismuller**, who went on to play Tarzan on film, was the first person to swim 100 m in less than one minute.
- **Captain Webb**, the first man to swim the English Channel, died when he drowned attempting to swim the rapids of the Niagara Falls.
- **The four strokes** used in international swimming competitions are the breaststroke, the crawl (freestyle) the backstroke and the butterfly.
- **Competitive swimming** is reputed to have started about 2000 years ago in Japan. It did not take off in Europe until the middle of the 19th century.
- **Eric Moussambani** became the first swimmer to represent Equatorial Guinea in the Olympic Games when he competed in the 2000 Sydney Olympics. Despite finishing last in a record slow time in the 100 m freestyle, he acquired the nickname of Eric the Eel.
- **The first heated swimming pools** were built in ancient Rome as early as 1BC.
- **On average, humans when swimming** can reach a top speed of 8 km/h, whereas fish have an average top speed of 108 km/h.

...FASCINATING FACT...

The ill-fated *Titanic*, which sank in 1912, was the first ocean liner to have a swimming pool on board.

Races and drivers

- **Races for track athletes** are always run anti-clockwise.
- **An annual pancake race** has been held in the town of Olney in the UK since 1445.
- **In the steeplechase track event** the water jump is cleared seven times with 28 obstacles being jumped in total.
- **The total distance run by horses** in the Aintree Grand National is 7.2 km, in the Epsom Derby it is 2.4 km and in the Kentucky Derby it is 2 km.
- **In dogsledding** a driver is called a musher.
- **Drivers first competed** in the RAC Rally in 1932; the name of the rally was changed in 1997 to Rally Great Britain.
- **Racing driver Niki Lauda** was administered the last rites as he lay dying after an accident in 1976. He recovered and was crowned world champion for the third time eight years later!
- **Contestants travel through** France, Spain, Morocco, Mauritania, Mali and Senegal in the Paris to Dakar Rally.
- **In ancient Rome** chariot races were contested over seven laps of the arena.
- **In the 2003 Formula One world championships** Michael Schumacher drove for Ferrari, Juan Pablo Montoya drove for Williams, David Coulthard drove for McLaren, Jacques Villeneuve drove for BAR (British and American Racing), Jarno Trulli drove for Renault, Giancarlo Fisichella drove for Jordan and Nicolas Kiesa drove for Minardi.

▲ *Jacques Villeneuve won the Formula One world championship in 1997.*

World football

- **Red and yellow cards** were first used by FIFA referees at the 1970 World Cup. Although numerous yellow cards were shown, not a single red card was brandished during the tournament.
- **In 1875 metal crossbars** were introduced for the goals. Previously a piece of tape had been used for a crossbar.
- **When England won the World Cup** in 1966 their mascot, a lion playing football, was called World Cup Willie.
- **Argentina's 1978 World Cup squad** included in its ranks a defender with the intimidating name of Daniel Killer.
- **In the first-ever World Cup** in 1930 the United States reached the semi-finals before losing 6–1 to Argentina.
- **The first British team** to win the European Cup was Celtic.
- **The African Nations Cup** was first contested in 1957 and was won by Egypt. Since then the tournament has been won most often by Ghana, with a total of five wins.
- **The phrase back to square one**, meaning back to the beginning, comes from football. Before football was televised, radio commentators divided the pitch into areas to describe to the listeners where the ball was. Square one was in front of the goals and if a ball went out of play for a goal kick, the commentator informed the listeners that the play was back to square one.
- **Chelsea were the first team** to field a side in a Premiership game composed of 11 foreign footballers.
- **The most recent winners of the European Nations Championships** have been France in 2000, Germany in 1996 and Denmark in 1992.

▲ *Italian forward Christian Vieri (left) and Angelo Di Livio argue with the referee as he gives out a red card to one of their teammates, Francesco Totti, during the 2002 FIFA World Cup.*

Ice hockey

- **The first-ever puck** used in a game of ice hockey was made from frozen cow dung.
- **An ice hockey puck** measures a thickness of 2.54 cm and a diameter of 7.5 cm.
- **Six players from each team** are allowed on the ice at any one time during play. The six positions are goalie, right defence, left defence, right wing, left wing and centre.
- **In 1925 in North America** the leading teams were known as the original six. They were: the Boston Bruins, the New York Rangers, the Chicago Blackhawks, the Montreal Canadiens, the Detroit Red Wings and the Toronto Maple Leafs.
- **Until 1971 the goalkeepers** in ice hockey were not allowed to fall to the ice to make a save.
- **An ice hockey rink is surrounded** by wooden or plastic walls known as the boards. These walls stand between 1.2 and 1.22 m in height
- **An ice hockey rink measures** between 26 and 30 m in width and 56 and 61 m in length.
- **The premier competition** in professional ice hockey is called the Stanley Cup and has been held every year since 1892, except for 1919 when it was cancelled due to an influenza epidemic.
- **Players skate around the rink** at speeds exceeding 50 km/h and the puck travels at speeds of over 150 km/h.
- **In ice hockey**, players who receive penalties or commit fouls are sent to the penalty box.

◀ *Ice hockey players have to control a puck whilst skating in all directions, including backwards.*

Football managers

- **Alex Ferguson became the first manager** to win a European trophy with both an English club and a Scottish club, achieving this feat with Aberdeen and Manchester United.
- **From 1996 to 2002** not one team with an English manager won the FA Cup.
- **Brian Clough** was sacked as manager of Leeds United after just 44 days, following a players' revolt.
- **Sven Goran Eriksson** became the 11th full-time England manager. His predecessors were Kevin Keegan, Glen Hoddle, Terry Venables, Graham Taylor, Bobby Robson, Ron Greenwood, Don Revie, Joe Mercer, Alf Ramsey and Walter Winterbottom.
- **Aston Villa** was the first team in England's top division to appoint a foreign manager when, in 1990, former Czech World Cup coach Dr Jozef Venglos took charge.
- **In the 2003/ 2004 season** the oldest manager in the premiership was Bobby Robson who celebrated his 70th birthday on February 18, 2003.
- **Franz Beckenbauer** was the first person to captain and coach a World Cup winning side. In 1974 he lifted the trophy for West Germany as captain and 16 years later he managed the German team to World Cup victory.
- **Bertie Vogts** became the first non-Scottish manager of Scotland. His first match in charge in 2002 ended in a 5–0 defeat against France.
- **When Kevin Keegan** was manager of Newcastle he made a TV advert for Sugar Puffs, which resulted in decreases in sales of the cereal in the area of local rivals Sunderland.

- **Three former England managers** left their Premiership teams during the 2002/2003 season. They were Terry Venables (Leeds United), Howard Wilkinson (Sunderland) and Graham Taylor (Aston Villa).

▲ *The England team go through their stretching excercises at a training session with Sven-Goran Eriksson before an Argentina match in 2002.*

Sporting terms

- **In cricket** an easy catch is known as a dolly, whereas in baseball it is known as a can of corn.
- **The sporting term** 'handicap' derives from horse racing. The riders of the best horses were made to ride with their caps in their hand.
- **Cover point**, fine leg, first slip, short leg, silly point and silly mid-off are all fielding positions in cricket.
- **If a horse wins a race** by a margin of 30 lengths or more this is known as having won by a distance.
- **The term** 'hang' ten is used in surfing. It means that the surfers stand at the front of their boards, gripping the boards with their ten toes.
- **In cricket scoring**, runs that are added from no balls, byes or wides are called extras. In Australia extras are known as sundries.
- **A toxopholist** is a technical term for a person who practises archery.
- **Five sports** that use a net but not a ball are ice hockey, fishing, badminton, the hammer and fencing.
- **In Gaelic football** the match takes place on a pitch known as the parallelogram.

▶ *A shuttlecock is hit when playing badminton.*

FASCINATING FACT

If a cricket batter fails to score any runs before he is dismissed, he is out for a duck. This term stems from a 1920s cricketer who owned a pet duck and was often out for zero whenever he took the duck to the game!

▲ *In ice hockey, when the puck is dropped between two opposing players to start or restart the game, it is known as a face-off.*

Rules of sport

▲ *Boxers are classified according to their weight and may not fight in a division lighter than their own.*

- **In volleyball**, rules state that the court should measure 18.2 x 9.1 m.
- **A set number of players** is required to form a team in each of these sports: five people for basketball, six for volleyball, nine for rounders, 11 for American football and 15 for hurling.
- **Boxing is governed** by the Queensberry Rules. When they were originally established they consisted of a list of 12 rules.
- **In discus competitions** the thrower may rotate up to four times and must not leave the throwing circle until the discus has landed.

- **In the game of croquet**, each ball must go through each hoop twice and strike the peg in the centre of the lawn. The ball is then removed from play and this is known as pegging out.
- **Swimming competitors** who jump back into the water after they have finished the race are disqualified if remaining swimmers have yet to finish.
- **The game of tennis** is controlled by an umpire who is assisted by foot-fault judges, net-cord judges and lines persons.
- **In football a goalkeeper** may not pick up or handle the ball from a deliberate back pass kicked by the foot. If any other part of the body is used when making the back pass then the keeper can use hands.
- **In the game of golf** a period of five minutes is allowed to search for a lost ball. If the ball is not found within this time another ball is used, but a one-stroke penalty is incurred.
- **The ten ways to be given out at cricket** are to be bowled out, run out, stumped, hitting the ball twice, obstructing the field, caught, LBW, timed out, handling the ball and hit wicket.

▶ *Natural hazards such as trees, water and sand-filled bunkers on golf courses make the game more challenging.*

Runners and running

- **British Olympic gold medallist** Sebastian Coe has the unusual middle name of Newbold.
- **The London Marathon** was first run in 1981 and 6255 of the 7747 runners who took part completed the course.
- **In 1986 the pop group Tears For Fears** released the song, 'Everybody Wants To Run The World' for the Sport Aid charity.
- **The maximum number of players** allowed on a cricket field during play is 15, consisting of 11 fielders, 2 batters and 2 runners. The runners come into play if a batter is injured and unable to run.
- **By tradition**, prior to the Olympic Games, the Olympic torch is carried by a collection of runners from Athens to the city hosting the Games. Every two years the Olympic flame is rekindled using strong magnifying equipment and the Sun's rays.
- **In international competitions** the longest foot race that is contested completely on the track is the 10,000 m, which works out as 25 laps of the track.
- **The longest track race** that is run solely in lanes is the 400 m. In the 4 x 400 m relay race, only the first leg is run in lanes.
- **In relay races the baton** must be exchanged in a 20 m takeover zone. If the baton is dropped, only the runner who drops it may pick it up.

▶ *The Olympic torch travels by runner to light the Olympic flame which will burn throughout the Olympic Games.*

- **Linford Christie**, who retired in 1997, now runs his own management company called Nuff Respect. Athletes that he now coaches include the 400 m runner Jamie Baulch, sprinters Darren Campbell and Katharine Merry, and hurdler Paul Gray.
- **In marathon races** the top athletes cover a distance of around 1.6 km every five minutes.

▶ *Running races have become a popular pastime for many people who want to stay fit and raise money for charity.*

Rugby

▲ *Rugby is a game of complicated rules in which the ball must be passed backwards or sideways, never forwards.*

> **...FASCINATING FACT...**
> In Rugby Union there are 15 players in each team while in Rugby League there are only 13.

- **The sport of rugby** started at Rugby School when a student called William Webb Ellis picked up the ball and ran during a game of football.
- **The city of Cape Town** in South Africa houses the largest Rugby Museum in the world.
- **There are four ways of scoring** in rugby: a try – worth five points; a conversion that follows a try – worth two points; a penalty goal – worth three points; and a dropped goal – worth three points.
- **The linesmen** in the game of rugby are called touch judges.
- **Eight forwards** from each team form a rugby scrum.
- **In Rugby Union**, the number shown on each shirt indicates the player's position. So, 1 and 3 are props, 2 is a hooker 4 and 5 are second rowers, 6 and 7 are flankers, 8 is the eighth man, 9 is the scrum half, 10 is the fly half, 11 and 14 are wingers, 12 and 13 are centres and 15 is the full back.
- **A rugby match** is played over two halves, each lasting 40 minutes, with a five-minute interval in between.
- **A rugby pitch** has maximum dimensions of 100 x 69 m and the longer sides are called the touchlines.
- **There are five teams** in the Tetley Superleague with names that include an animal: Bradford Bulls, London Broncos, Leeds Rhinos, Warrington Wolves and Castleford Tigers.

World records

- ***The Guinness Book of World Records*** is published in 23 different languages around the world.
- **The heaviest-ever** world boxing champion was Primo Carnera, who tipped the scales at 118 kg.
- **When Mark Spitz won** seven swimming gold medals at the 1972 Olympics he won all his races in world record times.
- **In 1998 at the age of 18 years and 62 days** Michael Owen became the youngest player to score a hat trick in the football Premiership.
- **The 1996 Superbowl** was the largest-ever TV audience to watch a game of American football. The Dallas Cowboys beat the Pittsburgh Steelers 27–17, watched by 138.5 million TV viewers.
- **In the year 2000 Manchester United** were officially named as the world's richest football club when they became the first club to have a market value exceeding £1 billion.
- **In the 20th century** the most-ever runners to finish a marathon race was 30,706 at the Boston Marathon in 1996.
- **The highest-ever test cricket batting average** of 99.94 is held by the legendary Sir Donald Bradman of Australia. In his final Test appearance he needed just four runs to give him a career average of 100 but unfortunately he was out for a duck.
- **Italian goalkeeper Dino Zoff** holds the record in international matches for keeping the most consecutive clean sheets. In the 1970s he kept goal for almost 13 matches, for a remarkable 1142 minutes, without conceding a goal.
- **In a 1999 cricket Test match** between New Zealand and South Africa, Geoff Allot batted for 1 hour, 41 minutes without scoring a single run.

◀ *In a spectacular year of achievements, Michael Owen was voted BBC Sports Personality of the Year in 1998.*

Card games

▶ *It was an ironic end for the famous gunslinger and prodigious gambler Wild Bill Hickok – he was shot dead playing poker!*

- **Playing cards** are thought to have originated in China after the invention of paper. Today a standard pack excluding jokers contains 52 cards, 13 of each suit.
- **Tarot cards** differ from standard playing cards as their suits are cups, swords, wands and pentacles.
- **Wild West hero** Wild Bill Hickok was shot dead playing poker, holding a pair of aces and a pair of eights. This hand is now known as a dead man's hand.
- **The top three hands** in a game of poker are; straight flush (top hand 10, jack, queen, king and ace of the same suit), four of a kind (top hand four aces), full house (top hand three aces and two kings).
- **The nine of diamonds** playing card is know as the curse of Scotland. One possible explanation is that the order given to carry out the Glencoe Massacre of 1692 was written on the back of this card.
- **The Bermuda Bowl** is presented to the winner of the men's bridge world championship. The female equivalent is called the Venice Trophy.
- **In packs of British playing cards** the queens that are depicted were inspired by Elizabeth of York, the wife of Henry VII.

...FASCINATING FACT...

The name given to a person that collects postcards is a deltiologist.

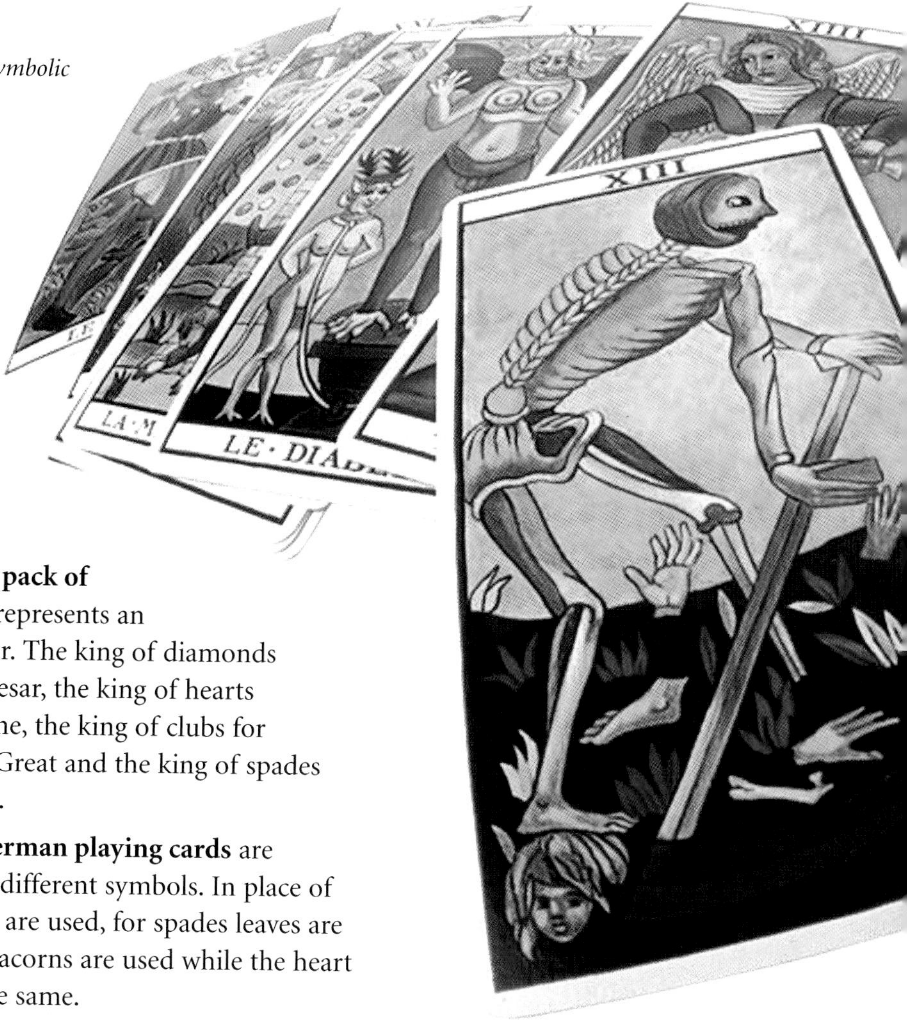

▶ *Tarot cards have symbolic illustrations that link to astrology.*

- **Each king in a pack of playing cards** represents an historical leader. The king of diamonds is for Julius Caesar, the king of hearts for Charlemagne, the king of clubs for Alexander the Great and the king of spades for King David.
- **The suits in German playing cards** are represented by different symbols. In place of diamonds bells are used, for spades leaves are used, for clubs acorns are used while the heart suits remain the same.

Wimbledon

- **The first ball girls** were not seen at Wimbledon until 1977.
- **The official name** of Wimbledon is the All England Lawn Tennis and Croquet Club.
- **The top three seeds** for Wimbledon in 2003 were: (1) Lleyton Hewitt, (2) Andre Agassi and(3) Juan Carlos Ferrero.
- **In 1996 at a rain-soaked Wimbledon** Cliff Richard sang a medley of his hits to entertain the fans.
- **Billie Jean King** is the oldest woman to receive a seed at Wimbledon, when at the age of 39 years, 209 days she received the No. 10 seed.
- **The winners of the men's singles** at Wimbledon receive a silver trophy that is inscribed with the words 'The All England Lawn Tennis Club Single Handed Champion of the World'.
- **The Wimbledon championship** is contested annually in the last week of June and the first week of July. The tournament was first covered by BBC Radio in 1927 and ten years later was shown for the first time on BBC Television.
- **In 1985 Boris Becker**, at the age of 17 years, 227 days, became the youngest-ever winner of the men's singles at Wimbledon. He was unseeded at the start of the tournament and was also the first German player to win the title.
- **Martina Navratilova** has won more singles titles at Wimbledon than any other woman. She won the title on nine occasions, including six consecutive victories from 1982 to 1987.
- **The main two courts** of Wimbledon are the Centre Court with a capacity of 13,806 and the No. 1 Court with a capacity of 11,428.

▲ *Wimbledon is one of the world's greatest tennis venues. It is one of the four major tournaments making up the Grand Slam in tennis.*

Skateboarding and snowboarding

- **When skateboarders** refer to the concave of a board they are talking about the way a board curves at the edges, tail and nose.
- **Snowboarders** leading with their right foot are known as goofy footed. A left leading foot is known as regular footed.
- **Snowboarding** made its debut in the Winter Olympics at Nagano in 1998.
- **In the giant slalom** in snowboarding, competitors use hard alpine boards to descend a downhill course travelling between gates. They are then judged on speed and technique.

▶ *Skateboarding developed in California in the 1960s and is a popular urban sport.*

...FASCINATING FACT...

Vert skateboarding is short for vertical skateboarding and involves skating up short steep curved walls. It originated in the 1960s in Los Angeles when a group of teenagers drained the water from a family swimming pool and skateboarded around the empty pool.

- **In 1999 Australian Darren Powell** created a new speed record for snowboarding, when his travelling speed was measured at 201.907 km/h.
- **In skateboarding** a kick flip involves kicking the board into a somersault, grabbing it in mid-air and replacing the feet on the board before it hits the ground.
- **Canadian snowboarder** Ross Rebaglaiti won the first Olympic gold medal for snowboarding in 1998.
- **Slamming** means falling off a skateboard and hurting oneself.
- **Snowboards are constructed** in four layers of different materials: the bottom layer is made of plastic with steel edges, the second layer is made of fibreglass that strengthens the board, the third layer is made of wood or foam and makes up the majority of the thickness, and the top layer is also made of fibreglass.

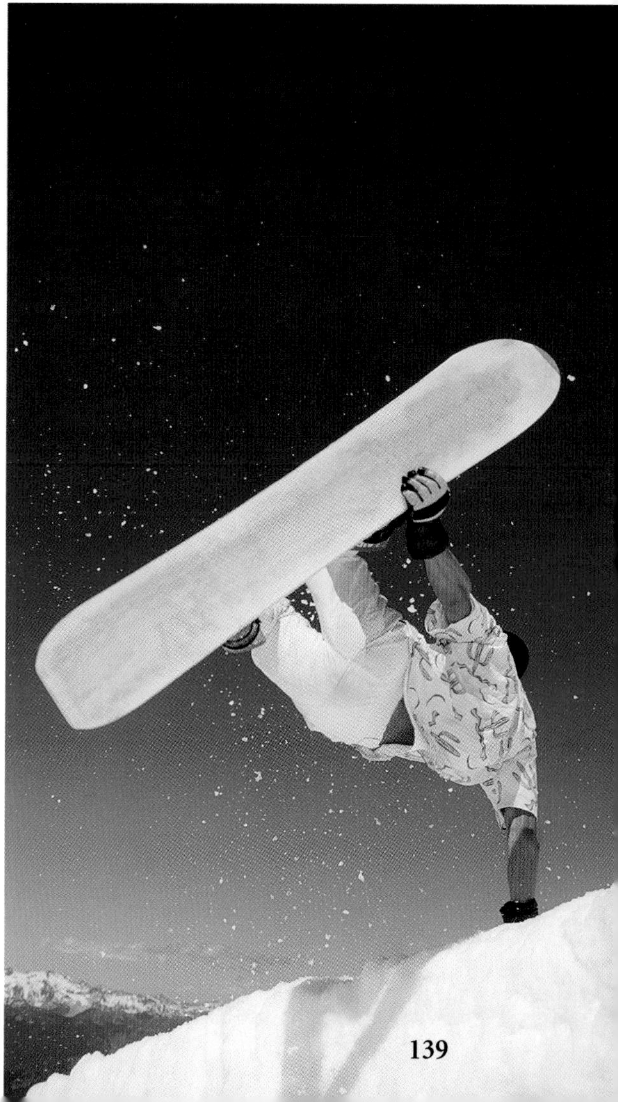

▶ *Snowboarding has become a popular recreational sport.*

The Summer Olympics

▲ *The last pure gold Olympic medals were awarded in 1912.*

- **At the first modern Summer Olympics** held in 1896 in Athens, 311 male athletes took part and no females.
- **In 1916, 1940 and 1944**, the Summer Olympics were cancelled due to World Wars I and II.
- **The opening ceremony** of the Olympics is always led by Greece, with the host nation marching out last.
- **Gold medallists** for the United Kingdom at the 2000 Olympics included Jason Queally for cycling, Denise Lewis for the heptathlon, Steve Redgrave for rowing, Iain Percy for sailing, Jonathan Edwards for the triple jump and Audley Harrison for boxing.
- **The first Summer Olympics** to be televised live were the 1960 Games hosted by Rome.
- **Recent events** that have been added to the Olympic programme include beach volleyball and mountain biking in 1996 and tae kwan do and women's weightlifting in 2000.
- **The term Olympiad** derives from the Greek language and means every four years.
- **Olympic athletes** were first tested for anabolic steroids at the 1976 Games in Montreal, Canada.

- **The tug-of-war** was an Olympic event from 1900 to 1920. In 1908 a team of London policemen won the gold medal.
- **Venues for the Modern Olympics**: 1896 – Athens, Greece; 1900 – Paris, France; 1904 – St Louis, USA; 1908 – London, UK; 1912- Stockholm, Sweden; 1920 – Antwerp, Belgium; 1924 – Paris, France; 1928 – Amsterdam, Holland; 1932 – Los Angeles, USA; 1936 – Berlin, Germany; 1948 – London, UK; 1952 – Helsinki, Finland; 1956 – Melbourne, Australia; 1960 – Rome, Italy; 1964 – Tokyo, Japan; 1968 – Mexico City, Mexico; 1972 – Munich, Germany; 1976 – Montreal, Canada; 1980 – Moscow, USSR; 1984 – Los Angeles, USA; 1988 – Seoul, South Korea; 1992 – Barcelona, Spain; 1996 – Atlanta, USA; 2000 – Sydney, Australia; 2004 Athens, Greece – where it all started.

▼ *Athens beat off rival bids from Buenos Aires, Cape Town, Istanbul, Lille, Rio, Rome, St Petersburg, San Juan, Seville and Stockholm to host the 2004 Games.*

Sportswear

- **In Rugby Union**, particular coloured shirts are linked to each national team. Gold is Australia's colour, white is England, France and Scotland both wear blue shirts, while Wales wear red and Ireland green.
- **Certain colours** are associated with particular football teams. Blue shirts are commonly worn by Italy, Scotland, France, Chelsea and Coventry, while red is the colour worn by Manchester United, Liverpool, Belgium, Spain and Wales.
- **The leotard costume** worn by trapeze artists was named after Jules Leotard, a 19th-century French acrobat who first wore one.

▶ *In gymnastics women tend to wear a leotard that is close-fitting leaving the limbs free for movement.*

- **The first FA Cup final** in which players wore numbers on their shirts was the 1933 final between Everton and Manchester City, with the players numbered from 1 to 22.
- **In 1990 FIFA** made the wearing of protective shin guards compulsory for footballers.
- **In fencing competitions** the fencers wear a protective mask, a metallic vest called a lame and a piece of material called a plastron that protects the chest and shoulders.
- **The football team** of Genk in Belgium is supported by fans who dress up as Smurfs!
- **The riding breeches** known as jodhpurs are named after the Indian city where they were first made, Jodhpur.
- **The 1915 FA Cup final** between Sheffield United and Chelsea became known as the Khaki final due to the large number of soldiers in the crowd.
- **The uniform worn** by a judo participant is called a judogi.

◄ *The judo player wears a white, loose-fitting jacket and trousers and performs barefoot.*

Sport in Europe

◀ *Zurich in Switzerland is home to the headquarters of FIFA.*

- **European teams** that have won football's World Cup are England, France, Germany and Italy.
- **Helsinki**, capital of Finland, is the most northerly city to have hosted the Summer Olympics.
- **In 1856 the Pau Golf Club** in France was the first golf club to be founded on the mainland of Europe.
- **The 1996 European Nations Championship** for football was held in England. The song 'Three Lions' was written by Frank Skinner, David Baddiel and the Lightning Seeds, especially for this tournament.
- **Tottenham Hotspur** was the first British club to win a European trophy when they collected the European Cup Winners' Cup in 1963.
- **FIFA**, the Federation of the International Football Association, has its headquarters in the Swiss city of Zurich.

... FASCINATING FACT ...

In the 1994 football World Cup, Bulgaria fielded a team of 11 players whose surnames all ended with the letters OV.

- **Weightlifting** is the official national sport of Bulgaria.
- **From 1977 to 1999** England, Ireland, Scotland, Wales and France contested the Five Nations Championship in Rugby Union. In 2000 this became the Six Nations Championship when Italy joined the tournament.
- **Despite France being ranked the No. 1** footballing nation in the world in 2002, the only French club to win the European Cup is Marseilles. They beat AC Milan 1–0 in the 1993 final, but were stripped of their title following a bribery scandal that involved Bernard Tapie, the club president.

▶ *Europe is still the most powerful continent in weightlifting competitions for both genders.*

Sport in literature

- **The author Mark Twain**, creator of *The Adventures of Tom Sawyer*, once described a game of golf as 'A good walk spoiled'.
- **The sport of baseball** was first referred to in 1803, in Jane Austen's book *Northangar Abbey*.
- **The author Bram Stoker**, the creator of Dracula, was an accomplished competitor in Victorian walking races.
- **Many autobiographies of footballers** have been published, including *My Side* by David Beckham, *Psycho* by Stuart Pearce, *Rock Bottom* by Paul Merson and *The Good, The Bad and The Bubbly* by George Best.
- **The back of an English £10 note** depicts a cricket match between Dingley Dell and All Muggleton, as described in Charles Dickens' novel *The Pickwick Papers*.
- **When Dick Francis**, a famous former jockey, retired from the sport he went on to write numerous bestselling novels set in the world of horse racing.
- **The novel *Fever Pitch*** is written by Nick Hornby and tells the story of an Arsenal fan who falls in love during their 1989 championship-winning season.
- **The game of billiards** was first mentioned in the world of literature in Shakespeare's play, *Antony and Cleopatra* when Cleopatra suggested to Charmian, "Let's to billiards".
- **The novel *National Velvet*** by Enid Bagnold tells the story of a 12-year-old jockey called Velvet Brown who rides a Grand National winning horse.

- **The novel *Harry Potter and the Philosopher's Stone*** features the wizard game of Quidditch. The four balls used in the game are a Quaffle, two Bludgers and the Golden Snitch. When the Golden Snitch is caught this is worth 150 points and the game is over.

▲ *The game of Quidditch in the Harry Potter books and films is played above a large field with the players on broomsticks.*

Bats and balls

. . . FASCINATING FACT . . .
The game of table tennis was originally played with bats made from the lids of cigar boxes and balls made from champagne corks.

- **The first golf balls** in the 16th century were made of wood. The following century they were made from goose feathers packed into a cowhide.
- **A regulation football** is made from 32 fabric panels held together by 642 stitches.
- **A golf ball** has dimples in order to maximize the distance a ball travels.
- **The Slazenger sports** company has been the official supplier of tennis balls for Wimbledon since 1902.
- **The sweet spot** is the name given to the point on a racket or a bat that vibrates the least when a ball is hit. When a ball hits the sweet spot it travels faster and farther.
- **In 1979 Australian cricketer Denis Lillee** came out to bat against England using an aluminium bat. The England captain Mike Brearly later complained that the bat was damaging the ball and Lillee was forced to replace it. Soon after the MCC introduced a law that all bats must be made from wood.
- **In the game of lacrosse**, a goal is scored when the ball is shot between two goal posts that are 1.8 m wide.

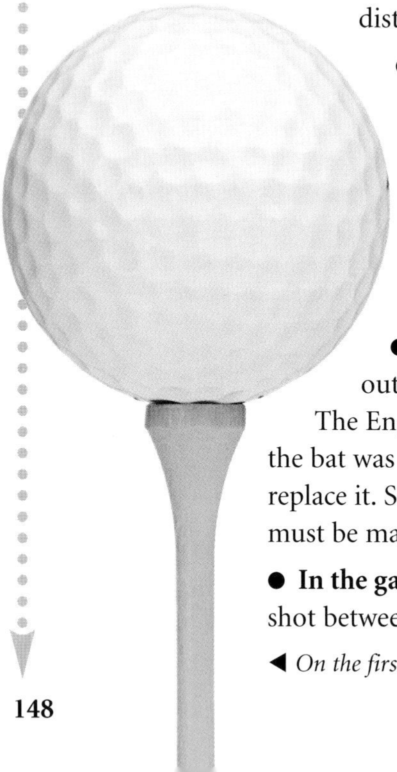

◀ *On the first shot at each hole the golf ball is hit from a tee.*

- **In the 1946 FA Cup final** between Derby County and Charlton Athletic the ball burst. Five days later, when Derby played Charlton in a league match, incredibly the ball burst again.
- **The diameters of various sporting balls** are 4 cm – squash ball, 4.26 cm – golf ball, 4 cm – table tennis ball and 5.24 cm – snooker ball.

▼ *Cricket balls have a circumference of 20.79–22.8 cm and weigh 155–163 g.*

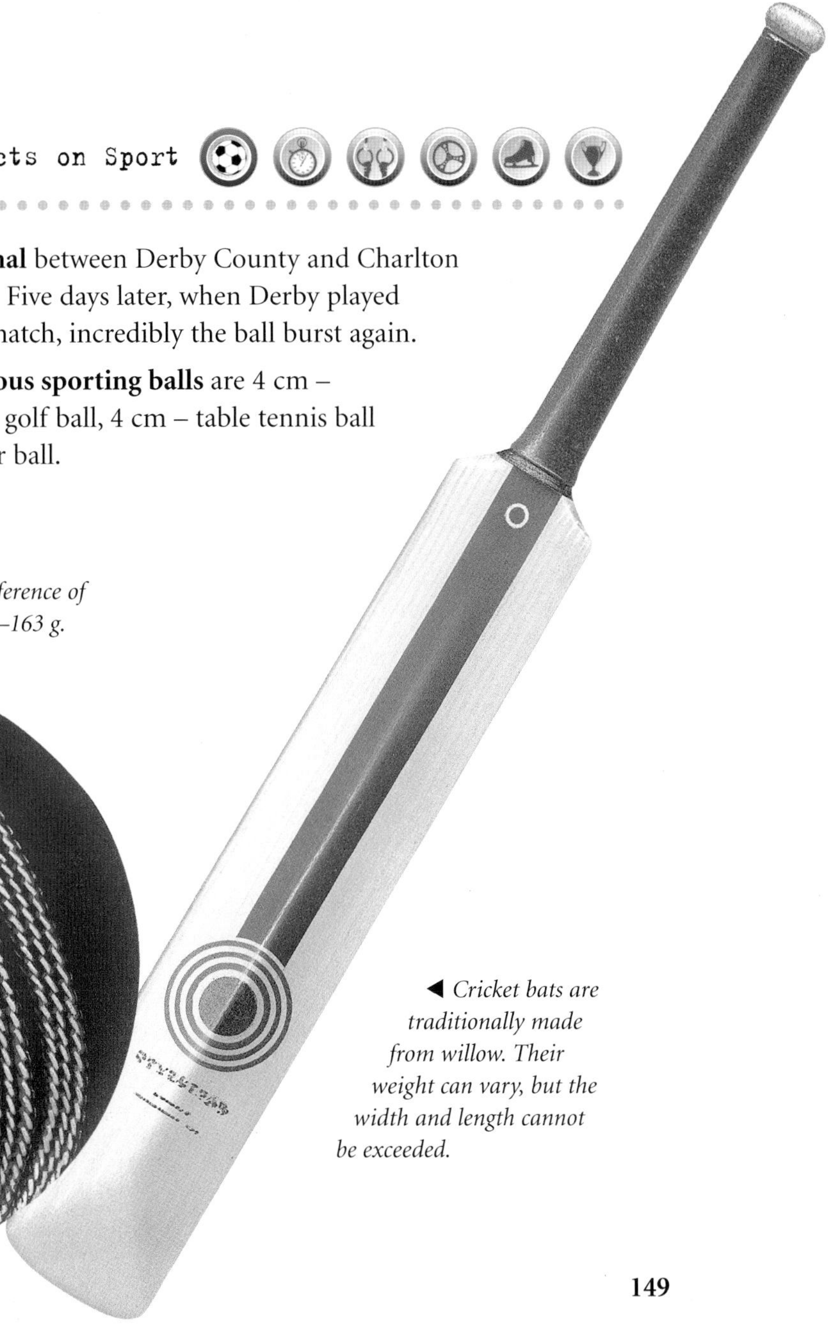

◀ *Cricket bats are traditionally made from willow. Their weight can vary, but the width and length cannot be exceeded.*

Manchester United

- **Manchester United** were originally called Newton Heath and were founded by a group of railway workers.
- **Between 1941 and 1949** Manchester United's ground, Old Trafford, was closed after it was bombed during World War II.
- **Bryan Robson** was the only player in the 20th century to captain three FA Cup-winning teams at Wembley, when he led Manchester United to victory in 1983, 1985 and 1990.
- **Striker Eric Cantona** played in 14 FA Cup ties for Manchester United without losing a single match.

▶ *Sir Alex Ferguson has shaped Manchester United into one of the world's top football teams.*

- **Ryan Giggs**, an international footballer with Wales, played schoolboy football for England under the name of Ryan Wilson.
- **Since 1960**, Manchester United has been managed by Matt Busby, Wilf McGuinness, Frank O'Farrell, Tommy Docherty, Dave Sexton, Ron Atkinson and Alex Ferguson.
- **In the 1999 European Cup final** the coloured ribbons representing Bayern Munich were tied on the trophy when the German club were leading in the final minute. They had to be hastily replaced when Manchester United scored twice in extra time to win the trophy.
- **Manchester United** are the only football club in Britain to have had a No. 1 hit record when, in 1994, they topped the charts with a song entitled 'Come On You Reds'.
- **Four Manchester United players** were named in England's 2002 World Cup squad. The players were Wes Brown, David Beckham, Paul Scholes and Nicky Butt. The squad also included ex-Manchester United star Teddy Sheringham.
- **Major honours won by Manchester United**: League champions – 1907/08, 1910/11, 1935/36, 1951/52, 1955/56, 1956/57, 1964/65,1966/67, 1992/93, 1993/94, 1995/96, 1996/97, 1998/99, 1999/00, 2000/01, 2002/03; FA Cup winners – 1909, 1948, 1963, 1977, 1983, 1985, 1990, 1994, 1996, 1999; European Cup winners – 1968, 1999; European Cup Winners' Cup – 1991; Football League Cup – 1992.

Symbols, logos and associations

- **The Olympic flag** is made up of five interlocking rings each representing a continent.
- **In 1997 Nike Sports Company** issued an apology for a new shoe logo, which was almost identical to the Arabic spelling of Allah.
- **In 2001 the WWF** (World Wrestling Federation, which is now called World Wrestling Entertainment) lost a court case against the WWF (World Wide Fund for Nature) over the use of the logo and initials WWF.
- **In Rugby Union**, the symbols representing each team are: red rose for England, shamrock for Ireland, thistle for Scotland and fleur-de-lis for Wales.
- **Six county cricket teams** have a flower on their badge. They are Lancashire, Yorkshire, Glamorgan, Hampshire, Surrey and Northamptonshire.
- **The horse-racing colours** for Her Majesty the Queen are purple and gold, with a black cap.
- **In skiing**, the slopes are graded by colour for difficulty. Green denotes a beginner's slope, blue an easy slope, red an intermediate or medium slope and black a difficult slope.
- **A roulette wheel** contains 16 red numbers, 16 black numbers and a green zero. Roulette wheels in the United States contain an extra zero.
- **What the initials stand** for in various sporting organizations: AAA – Amateur Athletics Association; MCC – Marylebone Cricket Club; BBBC – British Boxing Board of Control; EWCB – England and Wales Cricket Board; UEFA – Union of European Football Association.

▲ *At least one of the colours of the Olympic rings is represented in the flag of every participating nation.*

- **Symbols on badges of football clubs**: Blackburn Rovers – red rose; Arsenal – cannon; Leicester City – fox; Charlton Athletic – sword; Hull City – tiger; Coventry – elephant; Tottenham – cockerel; Plymouth – ship; Millwall – pair of lions.

Wrestling

▼ *Sumo wrestling is a traditional Japanese sport.*

- **Female wrestler Chyna**, whose real name is Joanie Laurer, became the first woman to compete in the Royal Rumble match at the WWF.
- **A Grand Champion** in sumo wrestling is called a yokozuna.
- **Before becoming an actor**, Tom Cruise was a keen wrestler and represented his college team.
- **The four officials** who control wrestling bouts in the Olympics are the mat chairman, the judge, the referee and the timekeeper.
- **The first WWE world champion** in 1963 was called Buddy Rogers. Other famous champions include Hulk Hogan, The Undertaker, Bret Hart, The Rock, Steve Austin, Triple H and Chris Jericho.

▶ *Wrestling attracts huge TV audiences.*

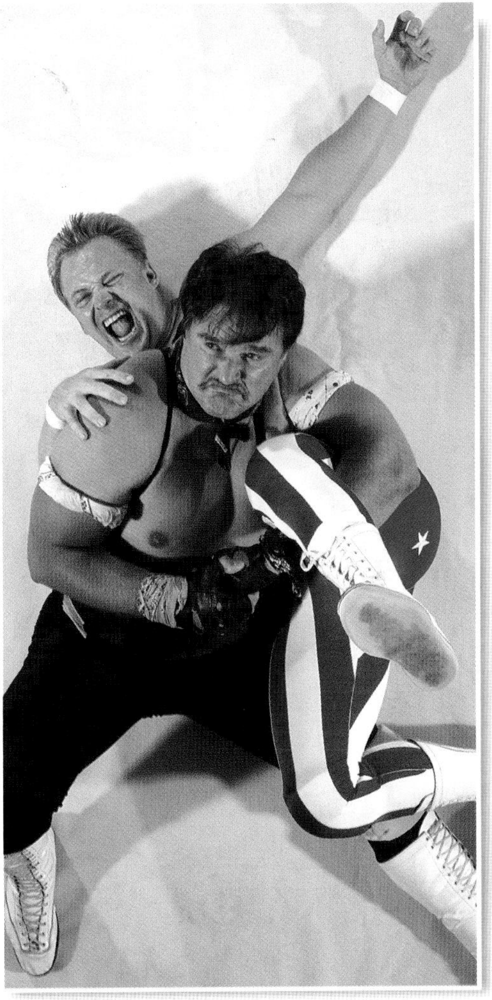

- **Wrestling** was an Olympic sport in the ancient Olympics and was also the last sport in the pentathlon.
- **WWE's headquarters** is in the town of Stamford in the American state of Connecticut.
- **To enter into the sport of sumo wrestling** a person must be at least 1.73 m tall and weigh a minimum of 75 kg.
- **The term** 'Its all fun and games until someone loses an eye' has its origins in ancient Rome. In wrestling contests the only way to be disqualified was to poke an opponent's eye out
- **Many wrestling stars** fight using nicknames. Big Boss Man is really Ray Taylor, Kane is Glen Jacobs, Stone Cold Steve Austin is Steve Williams, The Rock is Dwayne Johnson, The Undertaker is Mark Calloway and William Regal is Darren Matthews.

Royalty in sport

- **While attending Eton College**, Prince William was appointed captain of the school swimming team.
- **King George V** officially opened Wembley Stadium in 1923.
- **Mary Queen of Scots** had a billiard table in her cell, which she played on while awaiting her execution.
- **Princess Anne** was the first member of the British royal family to appear on a TV quiz show when she featured on *A Question of Sport.*
- **In the 18th century** Queen Anne founded the Ascot racecourse after buying an area of land for just £558. Today members of the royal family annually attend the Royal Ascot meeting, which opens with a race called The Queen Anne Stakes.
- **Crown Prince Constantin** of Greece won a gold medal at the 1960 Olympics for yachting.
- **Prince William** is a big fan of the Chicago Bulls basketball team, and has Michael Jordan's autograph.

▲ *King George V cut the first Wembley Stadium turf in 1923.*

- **The Duchess of Kent** is the royal patron of Wimbledon. When members of the royal family are present at Wimbledon tennis matches, the players bow and curtsy to them when leaving the courts.
- **In 1966 Queen Elizabeth II** presented the football World Cup to England Captain, Bobby Moore, at Wembley Stadium.
- **On July 30, 2002** Queen Elizabeth II officially opened the Commonwealth Games in Manchester.

▲ *A memorable time in footballing history as Queen Elizabeth II hands the Football World Cup to England's captain Bobby Moore in 1966.*

Sailing

- **Yachting** was due to make its Olympic debut in 1896 but was cancelled due to rough seas.
- **A catamaran** has two hulls and a trimaran has three.
- **For 132 years** the United States held the America's Cup in yachting before finally losing it to Australia in 1983.
- **In yachting**, a jib is a forward sail, the halyards are ropes for hoisting sails, the sheets are ropes for trimming sails and the spinnaker is a large triangular sail.
- **In December 2001** Ellen McArthur, aged 25, became the fastest woman to sail around the world in her yacht called *Kingfisher.*
- **On a yacht**, the long pole that secures the bottom of a ship's sail is called a boom. This pole swings to and fro and avoiding it is known as ducking the boom.
- **The right-hand side** of a sailing vessel is called the starboard and the left-hand side is called the port.
- **In yachting**, to change course away from the wind is known as gybing. Changing course towards the wind in known as luffing.
- **On June 27, 1898** Joshua Slocum became the first man to sail solo around the world. His voyage covered 74,000 km in a boat called *Spray* and lasted for more than three years.
- **The short chain**, or rope, that holds an anchor is called the painter.

◀ *It took 94 days for Ellen McArthur to sail round the world in her boat,* Kingfisher.

Sport at the movies

- **In the film** *Ace Ventura, Pet Detective,* Ace was hired to track down a dolphin, the mascot of the American football team Miami Dolphins.
- **Tom Hanks** played the manager of a female baseball team in the film *A League of Their Own,* with Madonna playing one of the team members.
- **Bobby Moore**, Pele and Ossie Ardiles all appeared in the film *Escape To Victory.* In this film Sylvester Stallone played the goalkeeper of the allies.
- **The 1981 film** *Chariots of Fire* told the true story of the British Olympic athletes Harold Abrahams and Eric Liddell, who won gold medals at the 1924 Games.
- **More films** have been made about boxing than any other sport.
- **In 1979 Hollywood film star Paul Newman** competed and actually finished second in the Le Mans 24-hour race.
- **In 2001 the actor Will Smith** portrayed the boxer Muhammad Ali in the film *Ali.* For a full year before filming began he prepared by jogging up to 8 km a day and taking part in boxing training for three hours a day.
- **In 2001 in the film** *The Mean Machine,* the footballer Vinnie Jones played an ex-professional footballer called Danny Meehan who was sent to prison and put in charge of the prison football team.
- **Is there any sporting activity** that James Bond does not excel at? In various Bond films he has demonstrated his expertise at a variety of sports including skiing, skydiving, mountaineering, snowboarding, golf, horse riding, motorcycling and ice-skating.

- **Opponents of Rocky Balboa**: *Rocky I & II* – Apollo Creed played by Carl Weathers; *Rocky III* – Clubber Lang played by Mr T; *Rocky IV* – Ivan Drago played by Dolph Lungren.

▲ *Sylvester Stallone starred in the successful* Rocky *movies in the 1970s.*

Sport in North America

- **Mushing**, which involves dogs pulling a sled, is the official state sport of Alaska.
- **The sport of lacrosse** originated in North America, and was played by North American Indians in preparation for war.
- **The 1976 Olympic Games** were held in Montreal in Canada and despite being the host nation, Canada failed to win a single gold medal.
- **The Commonwealth Games** were held in Canada in 1930 at Hamilton, in 1954 at Vancouver, in 1978 at Edmonton and in 1994 at Victoria.
- **In 1873 the first golf club** was founded in North America at the Royal Montreal Club in Canada.
- **In 1931 the famous Harlem Globetrotters** basketball team played an exhibition match in front of just one spectator. That person was Pius XI, who at the time held the position of Pope.

▼ *San Francisco, home of the famous 49ers American football team.*

- **Football is called soccer** (shortened from association) in North America in order to avoid confusion with the game of American football.
- **In 1980 Cliff Thorburn** became the only snooker player from North America to win the world title when he beat Alex Higgins 18–16 in the final.
- **One of the biggest ever shocks** in World Cup football came in 1950 when the United States beat England 1–0.

▲ *Huskies are a powerful breed of Arctic dog used to pull sledges.*

...FASCINATING FACT...
The San Francisco 49ers in American football were named after the gold prospectors of the 1849 gold rush.

Athletes

- **At the 1996 Summer Olympics** in Atlanta, 3543 female athletes took part.
- **At the 2001 World Athletics Championship**, triple jumper Jonathan Edwards won Britain's only gold medal.
- **In 1896 at the first modern Olympics** the winning athletes received a silver medal and a crown of olive branches.
- **British male athletes** who have won Olympic gold medals for the 100-m sprint are: Harold Abrahams in 1924, Allan Wells in 1980 and Linford Christie in 1992.
- **In 1972 the Finnish runner** Lasse Viren won the gold medal for the 10,000 m despite falling over during the race.
- **From 1972 to 1984** all athletes held the corner of their own national flag when taking the Olympic oath. Since 1984 the athletes hold the corner of the Olympic flag while taking the oath.
- **In 1971 Debbie Brill** became the first woman to jump 1.82 m (6 ft) in the high jump. She went on to dominate the event in the 1970s with her unique style of jumping known as the Brill Bend.
- **Since 1960** doves have been released at the opening ceremonies of the Olympics as a symbol of peace.
- **The track athlete Chris Chataway** won the first BBC Sports Personality of the Year Award in 1954. Other track and field athletes to have won the award include: Jonathan Edwards in 1995, Linford Christie in 1993, Liz McColgan in 1991, Fatima Whitbread in 1987, Daley Thompson in 1982, Sebastian Coe in 1979 and Steve Ovett in 1978.

FASCINATING FACT

The rules of the IAAF (International Amateur Athletic Federation) state that the maximum number of spikes allowed on athletes' footwear is 11.

▲ *British sprinter Linford Christie crosses the finishing line winning the 100-m sprint in Barcelona, 1992.*

The Winter Olympics

- **Eighteen Winter Olympics** were held in the 20th century, the first in 1924 in France and the last in 1998 in Japan.
- **The 2002 Winter Olympics** at Salt Lake City had three official mascots. They were a bear called Coal, a coyote called Copper and a hare called Powder.
- **No country in the Southern Hemisphere** has ever hosted the Winter Olympics.
- **The Winter Olympics** have been hosted by the United States on several occasions. In 1932 and 1980 they were held at Lake Placid, New York; in 1960 they took place at Squaw Valley, California; and in 2002 at Salt Lake City, Utah.
- **At the 2002 Winter Olympics** the Canadian team won the gold medal for ice-hockey beating their fierce rivals, the United States 5–2 in the final.
- **The Salt Lake City Winter Olympics** set the record for being the Games held at the highest ever altitude, at over 1300 m above sea level.
- **At the 1980 Winter Olympics**, the American speedskater Eric Heiden became the first person to win five individual gold medals at a single Games.
- **Up to and including the 2002 Games**, Norway has won the greatest number of Winter Olympic gold medals with a total of 94. In this time Great Britain has won just eight gold medals.
- **The Great Britain and Northern Ireland** women's curling team became national heroes in 2002 when they won the Olympic gold medal, beating Switzerland 4–3 in the final.
- **The 2006 Winter Olympics** are to be held in the Italian city of Turin. The last time Italy hosted the Games was in 1956 at the venue of Cortina d'Ampezzo. This venue inspired the name of the Ford Cortina car.

▲ *A victorious German ski-jumping team celebrate their gold medal win at the 2002 Salt Lake City Olympics.*

The Football League

▲ *Houghton (Villa) and Crawford (Blackburn) playing a match in 1910.*

- **The Football League in England** was founded in 1888, and the following year Preston North End became the first League champions.
- **The 12 founder members** of the Football League were Accrington Stanley, Aston Villa, Blackburn Rovers, Bolton Wanderers, Burnley, Derby County, Everton, Notts County, Preston North End, Stoke City, West Bromwich Albion and Wolverhampton Wanderers.
- **In 1993 the old Division One** became the Premier League, with Manchester United being crowned the first champions. The only other clubs to win the Premiership in the 1990s were Blackburn Rovers and Arsenal.
- **The first club** to win the League in three consecutive years was Huddersfield Town, from 1924 to 1926.
- **Manchester United striker Ruud Van Nistleroy** was the Premier League's leading goal scorer in 2002/03 with 25.

- **Five teams** who have completed the double (Football League champions and FA Cup winners in the same season) are Preston North End in 1889, Aston Villa in 1897, Tottenham in 1961, Liverpool in 1964, 1973 and 1988, Arsenal 1971, 1998 and 2002 and Manchester United in 1994, 1996 and 1999.
- **Since 1919 Arsenal** have never been relegated from England's Division.
- **In 1955 Chelsea** were the Football League champions, with the lowest-ever number of points, only 52 in total. This record is never likely to be repeated as in those days only two points were awarded for a win, as opposed to the three points awarded today.
- **Bolton, Fulham and Blackburn Rovers** were all promoted to the Premiership at the end of the 2000/01 season. They avoided relegation the following season and this was the first time in the history of the Premiership that all three promoted teams avoided relegation.
- **In 2002 Alan Shearer** became the first player to score 200 goals in the Premiership.

▶ *Newcastle captain Alan Shearer scores a penalty goal against Dynamo Kiev at a UEFA Champions League match in 2002.*

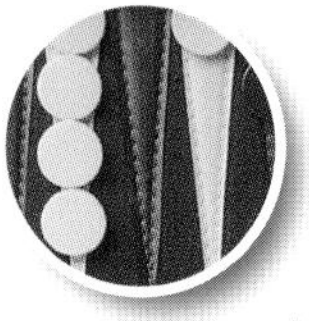

Board games

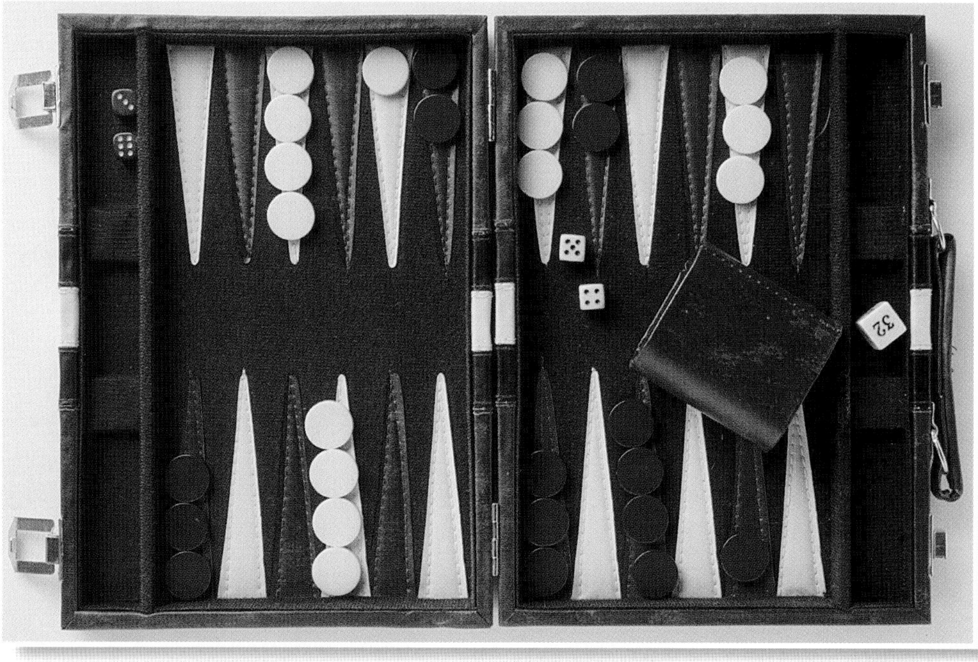

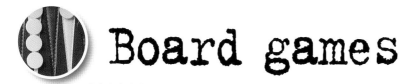

▲ *Backgammon is a game for two players.*

- **The ouija board** takes its name from the French and German words for yes.
- **The original Monopoly board game** was invented by a heating engineer and was based on the streets of Atlantic City in the United States.
- **In Scrabble** the total number of squares on the board is 225. The highest scoring letters are Q and Z, at 10 points each.

- **The murder suspects** in Cluedo are Miss Scarlet, Professor Plum, Mrs White, Colonel Mustard, Mrs Peacock and Reverend Green.
- **Lego was invented in Denmark** and its name in Danish means play well. In Latin the word 'Lego' means 'I put together'.
- **In a game of backgammon** each player starts with 15 pieces on a board that is divided into 24 dagger-shaped sections called points.
- **In the United States** the American equivalent of draughts is called checkers and the game of noughts and crosses is called tic-tac-toe.
- **The questions in Trivial Pursuit** are divided into six colour-coded subjects. The subjects are as follows: blue (geography), yellow (history), pink (entertainment), brown (art and literature), orange (sport and leisure) and green (science and nature).
- **The six murder weapons** in the game of Cluedo are a spanner, a candlestick, a revolver, a dagger, lead-piping and a rope.
- **On a Monopoly board** there are 22 different properties on which houses or hotels can be placed. In the British version of the game, the most expensive property is Mayfair. Boardwalk is the most expensive property in the American version.

▼ *Pieces from the game of Monopoly, the bestselling board game in the world.*

Umpires and referees

- **In cricket** one arm held out horizontally means the umpire is calling a no ball. Both hands held in the air above the head show that a six has been scored.
- **In 1991 Wendy Toms** became the first woman to officiate at a Football League match.
- **The umpires in baseball** are nicknamed zebras, because of the black and white shirts that they wear.
- **During a football match**, if the ball hits the referee and goes into the net a goal is given as he is considered to be part of the field of play.
- **At the ground of Yorkshire County Cricket Club**, the clock that stands above the western terraces is dedicated to the cricket umpire Dickie Bird.
- **In 1998 Paolo di Canio** received an 11-game ban and a £10,000 fine after he shoved the referee Paul Alcock to the ground during a League game.

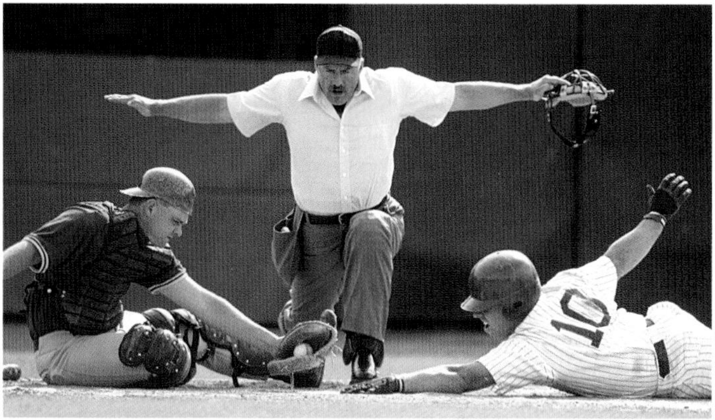

- **In 1972** a lady by the name of Berenice Gera became the first female baseball umpire.

◀ *The referee makes a decision in a game of baseball.*

- **Tennis umpires** are often met with abuse from temperamental players. They can actually issue warnings and deduct points for racket abuse should a player throw down his racket in frustration.
- **Graham Barber** lives on the same street as fellow Premiership referee Graham Poll. The pair once starred in a video explaining the rules of football.
- **Umpires and officials** at the Olympic Games have their own Olympic oath. It reads as follows, ‘In the name of all the judges and officials, I promise that we shall officiate in these Olympic Games with complete impartiality, respecting and abiding by the rules which govern them, in the true spirit of sportsmanship.’

◀ *Blowing the whistle during a game of American football.*

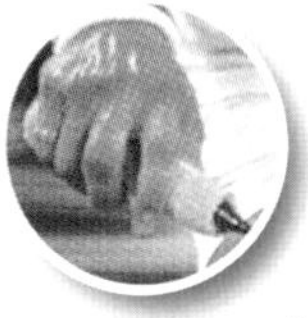

Badminton

- **The game of badminton** was named after the Gloucestershire home of the Duke of Beaufort, Badminton House.
- **In the Olympics** the rules state that shuttlecocks should have exactly 16 feathers.
- **The first player** to reach 15 points in a game, with a margin of at least two points, wins.
- **A badminton racket** must not be longer than 68 cm. The height of the net is set at 1.5 m.
- **In badminton**, points can only be scored off your own service.
- **Badminton** is the official national sport of Malaysia.
- **The International Badminton Federation** was founded in 1934 and in 1972 badminton became a demonstration sport at the Munich Olympics. The first Olympic gold medals for badminton were handed out at the 1992 Barcelona Games.
- **The rules of badminton** state that a shuttlecock should weigh between 4.74 and 5.5 g.
- **A badminton singles court** is 13.4 m long and 5.18 wide. A doubles court is 13.4 m long and 6.09 wide.

...FASCINATING FACT...

The best quality badminton shuttlecocks are said to be made from the feathers of the left wing of a goose.

◀ *In badminton the shuttlecock is served underarm.*

Football clubs

- **Crystal Palace** are the only Football League team whose name begins with five consonants.
- **Notts County** are the oldest League club in the world and were formed in 1862.
- **St Johnstone** are the only League team in England or Scotland with the letter J in the name.
- **Some football clubs** have changed their names. Birmingham City was originally known as Small Heath, Everton was known as Saint Domingo and West Ham was called Thames Ironworks Football Club.
- **Gillingham Football Club** are the only League club from the county of Kent.
- **Sunderland Football Club** were founded by a group of teachers and were originally called Sunderland and District Teachers Association Football Club.
- **In 1976 Wimbledon** were a non-League club. They gained entry into the Football League the following year, replacing Workington Town. Just 11 years later they won the FA Cup.
- **Leeds United** made their Football League debut in 1920; prior to that year they were called Leeds City.
- **In the 2002/03 season** English Football League teams had 20 different last names or suffixes. There were a number of teams with the last names of Town, United, City, Albion, Wanderers, Rovers, Athletic and County. Twelve teams had a unique last name: Aston Villa, Crewe Alexandra, Crystal Palace, Kidderminster Harriers, Leyton Orient, Plymouth Argyle, Preston North End, Port Vale, Queens Park Rangers, Rushden & Diamonds, Sheffield Wednesday and Tottenham Hotspur.

- **Frenchman Arsene Wenger** managed Arsenal to become League champions in 2002. He included five French players in the squad: Thierry Henry, Robert Pires, Patrick Viera, Sylvain Wiltord and Giles Grimaldi.

▲ *West Ham's Paulo Wanchope (left) is challenged by Tottenham's Stephen Carr during their Premiership match in 1999.*

Snooker

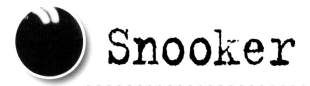

▲ *Snooker is now one of the most popular of all sports televised in Britain.*

- **There are 22 snooker balls** on the table at the start of the game: 15 red, one yellow, one green, one brown, one blue, one pink, one black and one white cue ball.
- **In 1990, at the age of 21**, Stephen Hendry became the youngest world snooker champion beating Jimmy White 18–12 in the final.
- **Each snooker ball** has a point value: one for red, two for yellow, three for green, four for brown, five for blue, six for pink and seven for black.
- **In order to make a 147 break**, a snooker player has to pot 36 consecutive balls.
- **A snooker table** is 3.65 m long and 1.8 m wide.

▲ *Stephen Hendry lines his cue up in a match.*

- **When Mark Williams** was crowned snooker world champion in 2003 he received the trophy and £270,000 prize money. The runner-up, Ken Doherty, won £158,000.
- **Steve Davis** made the first televised 147 break in 1982 in a tournament called The Lada Classic. His prize for achieving this feat was a brand new Lada car.
- **The final black ball** in the last frame settled the memorable 1985 world snooker final between Dennis Taylor and Steve Davis. A record TV audience of 18.5 million watched as Dennis Taylor potted the final black just after midnight to become world champion.
- **Stephen Hendry** has won the snooker world champion title most often: in 1990, 1992–1996 and in 1999. Other world champions are: Mark Williams in 2003, Peter Ebdon in 2002, Ronnie O'Sullivan in 2001, Mark Williams in 2000, John Higgins in 1998, Ken Doherty in 1997 and John Parrott in 1991.

FASCINATING FACT

The game of snooker originated in India in the 1870s where it was played by British Army officers. Cadets training to be officers were called snookers and this is where the name originated.

Goalkeepers

- **A goalkeeper** is allowed to hold onto the ball for no more than six seconds.
- **In 2001**, playing for Aston Villa, Peter Schmeichel became the first keeper to score a goal in a Premier League match.
- **When France won the World Cup** in 1998, Laurent Blanc kissed the bald head of Fabian Barthez prior to each game for good luck.
- **Goalkeepers** who have been voted Football Writers Player of the Year are Bert Trautmann in 1956, Gordon Banks in 1972, Pat Jenning in 1973 and Neville Southall in 1985.
- **The England football World Cup squad** for 2002 contained three goalkeepers: David Seaman, David James and Nigel Martyn.
- **In 1988 Dave Beasant of Wimbledon** became the first goalkeeper to save a penalty in an FA Cup final and also the first keeper to captain an FA Cup winning team.
- **Scottish goalkeeper Andy Goram** also represented Scotland in the game of cricket, playing in his first match against Australia in 1989.
- **In 1982 Italian goalkeeper Dino Zoff** became the first keeper to captain a World Cup winning team.
- **Prior to playing for Manchester City**, former England keeper David Seaman played for Arsenal, Queens Park Rangers, Birmingham City, Peterborough United and Leeds United.
- **In his early years Pope John Paul II** was a keen amateur goalkeeper and also excelled at swimming, canoeing, mountaineering and skiing.

▶ *English goalkeeper David Seaman during the match between England and Argentina in the 2002 FIFA World Cup.*

Horses in sport

- **Under Jockey Club Rules** 18 is the maximum number of letters allowed in the name of a racehorse.
- ***Red Rum*** is the only horse to have won the Grand National three times, in 1973, 1974 and 1977. He is now buried beside the winning post at Aintree.
- **The sport of skijoring** involves a skier being pulled by a horse.
- **The five 'classics'** in British flat racing are the 1000 Guineas, the 2000 Guineas, the Oaks, the St Leger and the Derby.
- **The three disciplines** in three-day eventing are showjumping, dressage and cross-country.
- **The film** *Champions* (1983) told the true story of Bob Champion, a former jockey, who overcame cancer to win the Grand National on *Aldaniti.*
- **In betting slang**, a pony is worth the sum of £25.

▼ *Jockeys wear identifying colours on their helmets and shirts. The colours are the property of the horse's owner.*

◀ *Polo is played between two teams of four people all mounted on horses.*

- **In 1993** ***Esha Ness*** was the first horse past the post in the Grand National but, due to a false start, the race was declared null and void and not rerun.
- **The English Grand National** is held at Aintree, the Scottish Grand National is held at Ayr, the Welsh Grand National is held at Chepstow and the Irish Grand National is held at Fairyhouse.
- **The name of the Derby horse race** rested on the toss of a coin. The organizers of the first race were the 11th Earl of Derby and Sir Charles Bunbury, and the Earl won the toss. If Sir Charles had won the toss the race would have been called the Bunbury Cup.

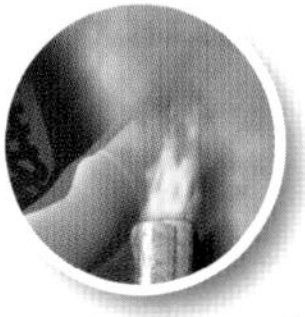

Sport on wheels

- **The Tour de France** cyclists cover a distance of more than 3400 km.
- **The only father and son** to have both been Formula One world champions are Graham Hill in 1962 and 1968 and Damon Hill in 1996.
- **Roller skates** were invented by a Belgian man called Joseph Merlin. The first time he used a pair in public he lost control and smashed a mirror at a masquerade ball.
- **The US Grand Prix** was originally held in Las Vegas in a giant parking lot.
- **Drag-racing contests** are started by an electronic device known as a Christmas tree, because of its multi-coloured lights.
- **A demolition derby** is a contest in stock-car racing. The drivers crash the cars into each other in an enclosed area until only one car is left running.
- **The British Grand Prix** in Formula One is run at Silverstone, which was originally used as a military airfield.
- **The engines of Formula One cars** must not exceed 3000 cc, and the cars are allowed a maximum number of 12 cylinders.
- **Michael Schumacher** became Formula One world champion in 2003, 2002, 2001, 2000, 1995 and 1994. Other champions have been Mika Hakkinen in 1999 and 1998, Jacques Villeneuve in 1997, Damon Hill in 1996, Alain Prost in 1993 and Nigel Mansell in 1992.

...FASCINATING FACT...

Race car is a palindrome, meaning it spells the same forwards as it does backwards.

▲ *A scene from the Playstation game* Destruction Derby, *based on the sport of demolition derby.*

Gold medals

- **In 1900 Charlotte Cooper** became the first woman to win an Olympic gold medal when she won the tennis tournament.
- **Olympic gold medals** are made mostly of silver. They contain 210 g of silver, which is coated with just 1g of 24 carat gold.
- **In 2000 boxer Audley Harrison** became the first British boxer since Chris Finnegan in 1968 to win an Olympic gold medal.
- **In the rowing events**, the British coxless-four team won a gold medal at the Sydney Olympics in 2000. The rowers were Steve Redgrave, Matthew Pinsent, Tim Foster and James Cracknell.

▲ *US swimmer Mark Spitz on the podium after winning the gold in the 100 m butterfly at the 1972 Olympics.*

- **At the 2000 Sydney Olympics** the American athlete Marion Jones became the first woman to win five medals at the same Games. She won gold in the 100 m, 200 m and 4 x 400 m relay, and two bronze medals in the long jump and the 4 x 100 m relay.
- **In 1988 the Canadian athlete** Ben Johnson set a new world record when winning the men's 100 m, but was disqualified when he tested positive for drugs. The gold medal was then presented to Carl Lewis.

- **The nations that won the most gold medals** in the 2000 Olympics were: United States – 40, Russian Federation – 32, China – 28, Australia – 16, Germany – 13, France – 13, and Italy – 13. At these Games the British team won 11 gold medals.
- **At the 2002 Salt Lake City Winter Olympics** all the medals were made from metal that was mined in the American state of Utah.
- **British middle-distance runner** Sebastian Coe won a gold medal in the 1500 m in 1980 and 1984, and went on to become a Conservative MP in 1992.

▲ *American athlete Carl Lewis finally ended his competitive career in 1997.*

- **Athletes who have won the most gold medals** in the Summer Olympics: 10 Ray Ewry, jumping events for the USA, 1900–1908; 9 Larissa Latynina, gymnastics for the USSR, 1956–1964; 9 Paavo Nurmi, long-distance runner for Finland, 1920–1928; 9 Mark Spitz, swimming for the USA, 1968–1972; 8 Matt Biondi, swimming for the USA, 1984–1992; 8 Carl Lewis, long jump/sprint for the USA, 1984–1982; 8 Sawao Kato, gymnastics for Japan, 1968–1976.

Bullfighting

- **The correct name** for a matador's cape is a *muleta*. It is red on one side and yellow on the other.
- **The colour red** means nothing to bulls as they are colour-blind.
- **Matadors** on horseback are known as picadors.
- **In bullfighting** a matador is the star bullfighter and the *toro* is the bull. A *traje de luces* is a sequinned suit worn by the bullfighter and a *veronica* is a type of pass where the cape is drawn over the bull's head.
- **The most expensive seats** at a bullfight are located in the shade.
- **Although bullfighting** is closely associated with Spain, many other countries stage bullfights. These include Egypt, Mexico, Portugal, France and Peru.
- **To start a contest** the President of the bullfight waves a white handkerchief to signal the entrance of the first bull into the ring.

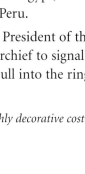

▶ *The bullfighter in his highly decorative costume and cape.*

- **Bullfighters wear colourful costumes** with the senior matador's costume decorated in gold. The colour yellow is never worn on a costume as it is considered unlucky.
- **A novice bullfighter** is called a *novillero* and fights in a contest known as a *novillado* with younger bulls.
- **Matadors wear a pigtail** that is clipped to the back of their head. When a matador gives up bullfighting the pigtail is cremoniously cut off in front of the bullfight crowd.

▶ *The American writer Ernest Hemingway wrote about bullfighting in his first novel* The Sun Also Rises *and later in* Death in the Afternoon.

The ancient Olympics

- **In the ancient Olympics** women were not permitted to watch the Games as the male athletes competed completely naked. The penalty for defying this rule was death!
- **The first-ever Olympics** was held in 776BC, and consisted of one sprint race which was won by a chef called Corubus.
- **The name of the Olympics** comes from Olympia, the city that first staged the Games.
- **The ancient Olympics** were held in honour of the Greek god, Zeus.

▲ *An old illustration showing early Greek youths competing in different sports.*

- **Only Greek athletes** that were free citizens were allowed to compete in the ancient Olympics.
- **The Pankration** was a contest that was a combination of no-holds barred wrestling and boxing in which kicking was allowed. Two separate events were contested, one for young boys and one for men.
- **Winning athletes** at the ancient Olympics received a crown made from olive leaves and they were also entitled to have a statue erected in their honour at the Olympia site.

- **When training for the ancient Olympics** the athletes often exercised to the sound of flute music, as the Greeks believed that this helped to improve co-ordination and movement.
- **In 680BC**, chariot races were introduced in which riders raced over a distance of 14.4 km in a stadium called a hippodrome.
- **The ancient Olympics** were held over a 1000-year period. In AD400 the sacred shrine at Olympia, which hosted the Games, was destroyed and the following year the Roman Emperor abolished the Games.

▶ *Chariots were used for processions, fighting or races in ancient Egypt, Rome and Greece. It is thought that they originated in Asia.*

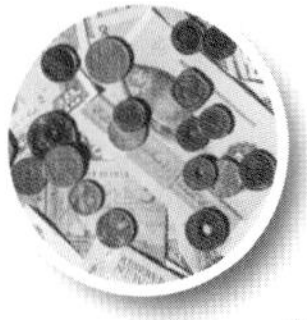

Football transfers

- **The first British player** to be transferred for £1000 was Alf Common from Sunderland to Middlesbrough. David Jack was the first player to be transferred for £10,000 from Bolton to Arsenal. Trevor Francis was the first player to be transferred for £1 million from Birmingham to Nottingham Forest and Chris Sutton was the first player to be transferred for £5 million from Norwich to Blackburn Rovers.
- **Jimmy Greaves** was signed by Tottenham from AC Milan.The fee was £99,999 as he did not want to become the first £100,000 player.
- **The first goalkeeper** to be transferred for £1 million was Nigel Martyn when Leeds bought him from Crystal Palace.
- **To date the record transfer fee** paid by a British club for a teenager is £6 million, when Coventry bought 19-year-old Robbie Keane from Wolves in 1999.
- **In 1990 a Belgium footballer** called Jean-Marc Bosman took his club RC Liege to court, claiming they had prevented his transfer to a French club. He won his case, which means that players in Europe can now move to another club without a transfer fee at the end of their contracts. This has become known as the Bosman Ruling.
- **The record fee received** by a British club in the 20th century was £22.5 million, when Arsenal sold Nicholas Anelka to Real Madrid in 1999.
- **Transfers involving the striker Clive Allan** took him to Queens Park Rangers, Arsenal, Crystal Palace, Spurs, Manchester City, Bordeaux, Chelsea, West Ham, Millwall and Carlisle United. He also played as a goal kicker for the London Monarchs and now works for Sky Sports as a TV pundit

◀ *Manchester United's Rio Ferdinand (left) is challenged by Ronaldo in a match in 2003.*

- **In 2001 Real Madrid** paid a world record fee of £45.62 million for Zinedine Zidane.
- **In the summer of 1995** Manchester United sold their star mid-fielders Paul Ince and Andrei Kanchelskis. A pair of promising youngsters replaced them by the names of Paul Scholes and David Beckham.
- **Up to January 2004** the most money paid by a Premiership club to sign up a player was £29.1 million paid by Manchester United for Rio Ferdinand.

European football

- **The Spanish club Real Madrid** dominated the early years of the European Cup, winning the first five tournaments from 1956 to 1960.
- **Juventus were Italy's champions for 2003**. Other League champions in that year were Real Madrid in Spain, Bayern Munich in Germany, Lyon in France and Porto in Portugal.
- **The Italian club Juventus** adopted their black and white shirt from the English club Notts County.
- **The only four English clubs** to have won the European Champions Cup are Manchester United, Liverpool, Aston Villa and Nottingham Forest.
- **The Newcastle manager Bobby Robson** has enjoyed successful spells as manager of clubs on mainland Europe. He has coached PSV Eindhoven in Holland, FC Porto and Sporting Lisbon in Portugal, and Barcelona in Spain.
- **The only three clubs** to have won the European Champions Cup in three consecutive years are Real Madrid, Ajax and Bayern Munich.
- **The winners of the European Super Cup** between 1991 and 2003 are: Manchester United (1991), Barcelona (1992), Parma (1993), Milan (1994), Ajax (1995), Juventus (1996), Barcelona (1997), Chelsea (1998), Lazio (1999), Galatasaray (2000), Liverpool (2001), Real Madrid (2002) and Milan (2003).
- **Football is a major sport in Italy**. Some local derbies played there are the Milan Derby (Inter Milan v AC Milan), the Turin Derby (Juventus v Torino) and the Rome Derby (Lazio v Roma).
- **In England the top teams play in the Premier Division**. In Italy this is called Serie A, in Spain it is called La Liga and in Germany it is called Bundesliga.

- **The Football League competition in Spain** began in 1928 and was suspended from 1936 to 1939 due to the Spanish Civil War. By the end of the 20th century Real Madrid had won the title 28 times and Barcelona had won it 15 times. These are the only teams that played in every single season.

◀ *Real Madrid's David Beckham vies with Gonzalez (left) of Mallorca in a match in 2003.*

Throwing

◀ *A shot put is made of metal and weights vary for women and men competitors. The shot is thrown from a throwing circle.*

- **Javelins must be** between 2.6 and 2.7 m in length for men's competitions and between 2.2 and 2.3 m in length for women's competitions.
- **In football** if the ball passes into the net from a throw-in without touching another player then a goal kick is awarded.
- **Javelins were made of wood** until 1950 when an aluminium javelin was designed that enabled throwers to achieve greater distances.
- **The official weight of the men's discus** is 2 kg, and for the women's is 1 kg. The men's javelin must weigh 800 g to the women's 600 g. The shot-put must weigh 7.26 kg for the men and 4 kg for the women.
- **In the game of quoits**, the players, known as quoiters, throw round discs with a hole in the centre over a vertical stake or pin sticking out of the ground.

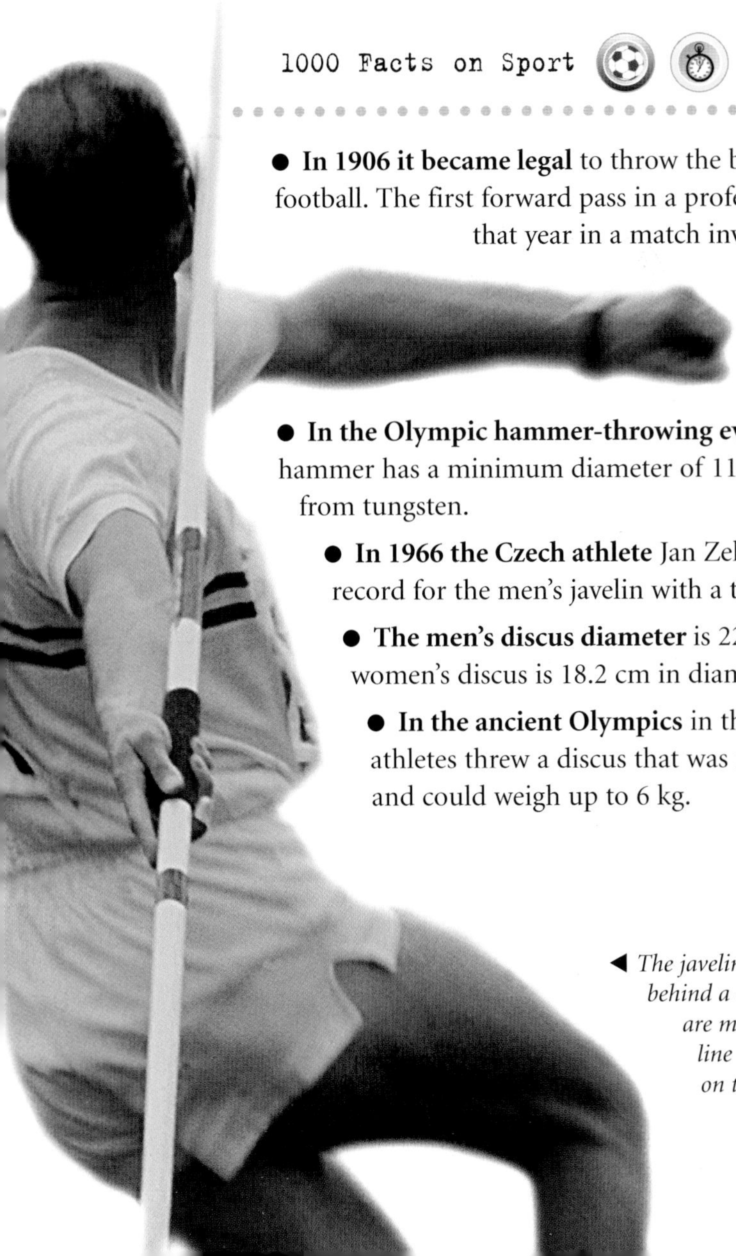

● **In 1906 it became legal** to throw the ball forward in American football. The first forward pass in a professional game was made that year in a match involving two teams called Benwood-Moundsville and Massillon.

● **In the Olympic hammer-throwing event,** the head of the hammer has a minimum diameter of 110 mm and is made from tungsten.

● **In 1966 the Czech athlete** Jan Zelezny set a new world record for the men's javelin with a throw of 98.48 m.

● **The men's discus diameter** is 22 cm in diameter. The women's discus is 18.2 cm in diameter.

● **In the ancient Olympics** in the discus event, the athletes threw a discus that was made of stone or bronze and could weigh up to 6 kg.

◀ *The javelin is thrown overarm from behind a curved white line. Distances are measured from the throwing line to the nearest mark made on the ground by the javelin.*

Darts

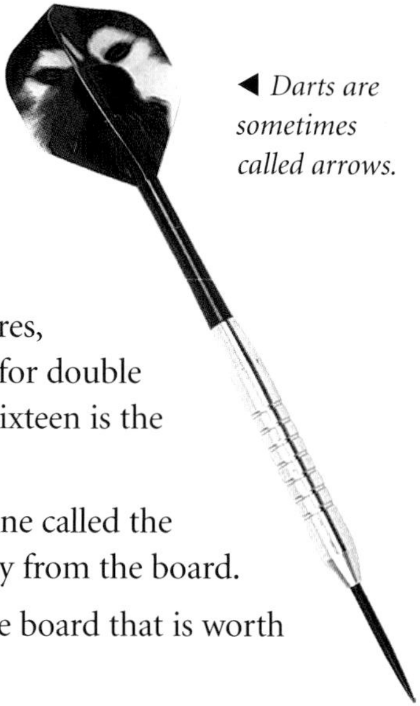

◀ *Darts are sometimes called arrows.*

- **Dartboards** are made from sisal, wood or wound paper.
- **The lowest number** that is impossible to score with one single dart is 23.
- **The highest check out** with three darts is 170, two treble 20s and a bull's-eye.
- **In darts** there are special terms for particular scores, namely double top for double 20, the madhouse for double one and the basement for double three. Double sixteen is the most popular double to finish on.
- **In professional darts**, the players throw from a line called the oche (pronounced 'ockey') that stands 2.3 m away from the board.
- **On a dartboard** the bull's-eye is the section of the board that is worth 50 points and has a diameter of just 8 mm.
- **Darts has been played in England** since the Middle Ages, and the board was originally a cask of ale turned onto its side. *The Mayflower* that took the Pilgrim Fathers to America was said to have a dartboard on board.
- **The first darts world championship** was held in 1978 and was won by Leighton Rees of Wales. Today, the top player is Phil Taylor who narrowly missed winning his 11th title in 2003.
- **In professional darts matches** the players start with a score of 501 and work backwards finishing on a double or the bull's-eye. A perfect game is a nine-dart finish and the first person to achieve this feat on television was John Lowe. His first six darts all hit the treble 20 leaving him with 141. He then finished with a treble 17, a treble 18 and a double 18.

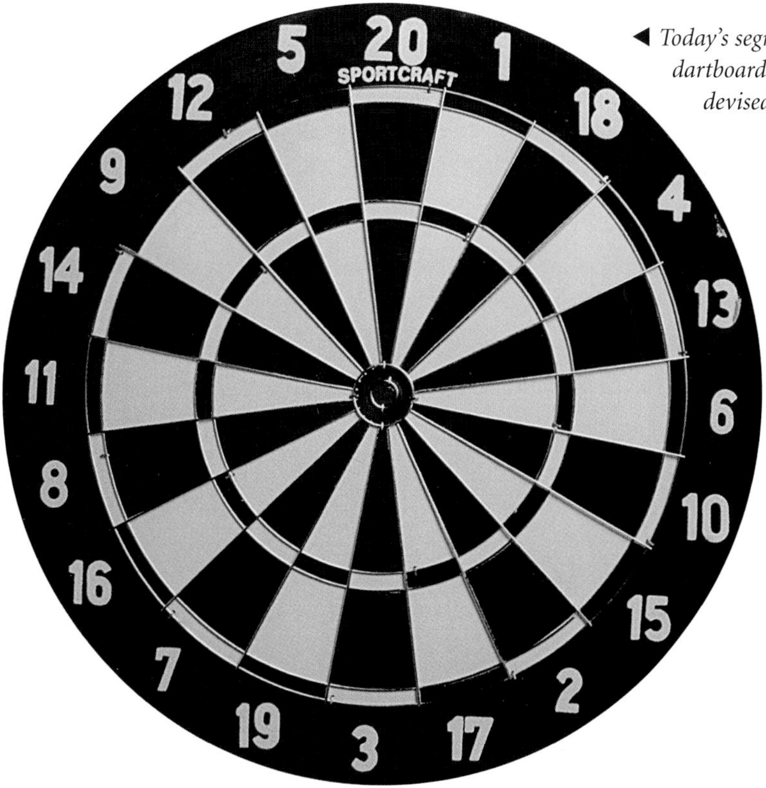

Today's segmented dartboard was devised in 1896.

...FASCINATING FACT...

The name for the game of darts originated from the word 'dhart', which was an ancient word for a spear.

Football in Scotland

- **Berwick Rangers** are the only English team to play in the Scottish League.
- **Celtic play at Celtic Park**, Rangers at Ibrox Park, Dundee at Dens Park, Dundee United at Tannadice Park and Aberdeen at Pittodrie Stadium.
- **In 1967 Celtic** became the first British club to win the European Cup, beating Inter Milan 2–1 in the final.
- **Some teams have nicknames**. Celtic are known as the Bhoys, Rangers as the Gers, Ayr United as the Honest Men, Hearts as the Jam Tarts and Clyde as the Bully Wee.
- **In 2000**, Elgin City and Peterhead were the latest teams to be elected into the Scottish League.
- **In 2002 Celtic won** their 36th Scottish League title. However the other Glasgow team, Rangers, have won the most Scottish titles with a total to date of 49.
- **Of the first ten Scottish Cup finals**, Queen's Park, Scotland's oldest League club, won six.
- **In 1909 Celtic and Rangers** contested the Scottish Cup final. The first game ended in a 2–2 draw and the second game was abandoned in extra time with the score at 1–1 after the crowd rioted. Both teams refused to play a third match and the cup was withheld that year.

...FASCINATING FACT...

The Scottish teams East Stirlingshire and Inverness Caledonian Thistle are the only two League teams in England or Scotland to have three letter S's in their name.

- **From 1980 to 2002**, the only teams other than Celtic or Rangers to win the League title in Scotland's top division were Aberdeen and Dundee United. The Aberdeen manager at the time was Alex Ferguson.

▲ *Playing at Celtic Park in Glasgow, Celtic's Alan Thompson (right) with Jezdimirovics Goran and Komlusi Adam during their Champions League qualifying match in 2003.*

Cycling

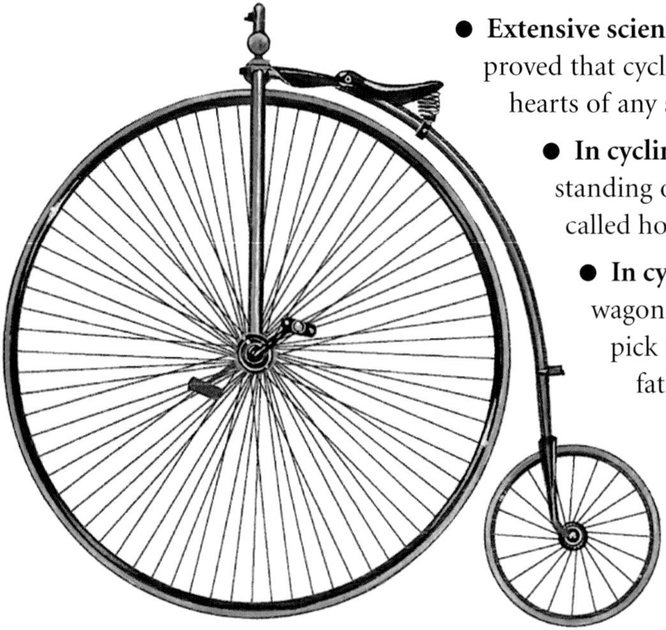

▲ *The first bicycle, a form of hobby-horse, was seen in Paris in 1791. By the end of the 19th century the penny farthing had evolved.*

- **Extensive scientific research** has proved that cyclists have the largest hearts of any sports competitors.
- **In cycling**, the practice of standing out of the saddle is called honking.
- **In cycle races** a sag wagon is employed to pick up injured or fatigued cyclists.
- **The leader and eventual winner** in the Tour de France is presented with a yellow jersey. A white jersey is awarded to the best rider under the age of 25.
- **In 1986 the American cyclist** Greg LeMond became the first non-European to win the Tour de France.
- **Cycling was contested** in the first modern Olympics of 1896 and the first road race was over a distance of 87 km.
- **The first-ever mountain biking world championship** was held in the American state of Colorado in 1990.

- **The name BMX** for bicycles is short for Bicycle Moto Cross.
- **In the 1990s** the Spanish cyclist Miguel Indurain became the first cyclist to win the Tour de France for five years in a row.
- **In the 19th century** a bicycle was introduced called a penny-farthing, which had a large front wheel and a small back wheel. It got its name because it resembled a large old penny coin next to a farthing coin.

▶ *A poster advertising a cycle race.*

▼*Modern materials and technologies have created faster bicycles.*

Other sports

- **The sporting body USLMRA** is the ruling body of the US Lawn Mower Racing Association.
- **The Sheikh Zayed President's Cup** is a leading event in camel racing.
- **At the 1908 London Olympics** a team of London policemen won the gold medal for the tug-of-war.
- **The appropriately named Richard Flicker** is a past England junior champion at the game of Subbuteo.
- **A frisbee** was originally called a Pluto Platter.
- **Spelunkers or speleologists** are people who explore caves or potholes.

▲ *Marbles have been around for thousands of years – examples have been found in archaeological sites all over the world.*

- **In the game of tiddlywinks**, the smaller counters are the winks and the large counter that flips the winks is called a squidger.
- **In the sport of barrel jumping** ice-skaters travel at speeds approaching 50 km/h before attempting to leap over as many barrels as possible.
- **In marbles**, the marble used for shooting is called a taw, and the marble being shot at is called the duck.
- **The sport of base jumping** involves leaping off high buildings with a parachute. Base stands for building, antennae, span and earth.

▲ *Tug-of-war contests are governed by strict rules of play. The person at the end of the rope is known as the anchor.*

Unusual sports

- **The village green** of Ashton in England hosts the World Conker Championships every October.
- **The World Gurning Championships** are held at the Egremont Crab Fair in the Lake District. The contestants put their head through a horse collar and whoever pulls the funniest or ugliest face is declared champion.
- **In the village of Brockworth** in Gloucestershire regular cheese-chasing contests are held, where the contestants attempt to catch a large cheese rolling down a steep hill. The local council have in the past tried to ban the event because of the number of injuries sustained.
- **The state of New South Wales** in Australia hosts the annual World Egg Throwing Championships. The contestants attempt to throw eggs over a 40-m high building and the eggs have to be caught by a partner on the other side without breaking.
- **In the country of Nepal** the game of polo is played using elephants instead of horses.
- **The game of underwater rugby**, popular in Germany, is played in a swimming pool and tries are scored by placing the ball in a round metal basket at the bottom of each end of the pool.
- **The Finnish town of Sonkajarvi** hosts an annual wife-carrying contest, with the first past the winning post in the fastest time being the winner.

▶ *Prizes such as a silver tankard stuffed with lettuce leaves are offered as an incentive to participants in snail races.*

- **The town of Llantwrtyd Wells in Wales** holds an annual Man Versus Horse Marathon over a distance of 35 km. The human contestants get a 15-minute start on the horses and £10,000 prize money is given to any runner that beats the leading horse.
- **In 1995 a new world record** of two minutes over a distance of 33 cm was set by a garden snail called Archie in the World Snail Racing Championships.
- **Bog or ditch snorkelling** is popular in East Anglia. Competitors wearing a mask and flippers attempt to make progress through a peat bog in the fastest possible time.

▲*These bog-snorkellers are required to complete two lengths of a 65-m trench cut through a peat bog in the quickest time possible without using conventional swimming strokes.*

Index

Index

Index

G

H

Index

Index

Index

P

Q

R

S

Index

T

Index

XYZ

Acknowledgements

The publishers would like to thank the following artists who have contributed to this book:
Nicholas Forder, Terry Gabbey, Rob Jakeway, John James (Temple Rogers), Janos Marffy, Massimiliano Maugeri, Andrea Morandi, Martin Sanders, Peter Sarson, Guy Smith, Rudi Vizi, Mike White (Temple Rogers)

The publishers would like to thank the following sources for the use of their photographs:
Page 9 Pornchai Kittiwong Sakul/AFP/Getty Images; 14 Emmanuel Dunand/AFP/Getty Images; 21 Corr-Cor/AFP/Getty Images; 29 AFP/Getty Images; 37 Jack Guez/AFP/Getty Images; 41 Central Press/AFP/Getty Images; 67 STAFF/AFP/Getty Images; 71 Kevin Fleming/CORBIS; 75 AFP/Getty Images; 81 Gordon Brooks/AFP/GettyImages; 83 Ji Ji Press-off/AFP/Getty Images; 85 Jeff Haynes/AFP/Getty Images; 87 Antonio Scorza/AFP/Getty Images; 91 William West/AFP/Getty Images; 98 Franck Fife/AFP/Getty Images; 101 AFP/Getty Images; 109 Kim Jae-Hwan/AFP/Getty Images; 112 William West/AFP/Getty Images; 119 Kim Jae-Hwan/AFP/Getty Images; 123 William West/AFP/Getty Images; 129 Gerard Kelly; 133 Kazuhiro Nogi/AFP/Getty Images; 147 Warner Bros/Pictorial Press; 150 Adrian Dennis/AFP/Getty Images; 157 STAFF/AFP/Getty Images; 159 Martyn Hayhow/AFP/Getty Images; 161 UA/Irwin Winkler/Pictorial Press; 165 Eric Feferberg/AFP/Getty Images; 167 Oliver Multhaup/AFP/Getty Images; 169 Odd Andersen/AFP/Getty Images; 177 Sinead Lynch/AFP/Getty Images; 179 Pornchai Kittiwong Sakul/AFP/Getty Images; 181 Toshifumi Kitamura/AFP/Getty Images; 185 Sony Computer Entertainment; 186 STAFF/AFP/Getty Images; 189 Pictorial Press; 193 Pierre-Philippe Marcou/AFP/Getty Images; 195 Javier Soriano/AFP/Getty Images; 201 Ian Stewart/AFP/Getty Images; 207 Chris Prichard

Castrol, MCD Library, Corbis, Corel, digitalSTOCK, digitalvision, Hemera, ILN, PhotoAlto, PhotoDisc

All other photographs from Miles Kelly Archives